CW00537670

INSPIRED GRAZING

CHEESEBOARDS & SHARING PLATES FOR ALL SEASONS

LAURA BILLINGTON

CONTENTS

Spring

Summer

Autumn

Winter

The Pantry

THANK YOU

To Neil, my husband, who always supports me and is my biggest encourager. I love you. You inspire me to be better every day.

To my mum and dad, who taught me to follow my dreams and to do whatever makes me happy.

To my three daughters, Nicole, Natalie & Niamh, who inspire me every day, with a very special thank you to Nicole for the illustrations in this book. You all mean the world to me.

To Meze Publishing for believing in this book, especially Phil who listened to me drone on about the book and agreed to publish it.

To Katie, the most patient and talented editor with an amazing eye and attention to detail.

To Paul for always listening, offering advice, joyful phone chats on life and allowing my creativity to shine through, but for also being creative and designing this book just how I envisaged it.

To Emma for all the publicity, passion, sales expertise and help she has given and to the rest of the team for bringing this book together. I simply will never be able to thank you enough.

To Jenny and Danny Shortall, for your patience, your creativity, your commitment and most of all your talent and expertise because without the photographs, this book would not exist. Thank you for always listening to me, evolving with me and helping me become better in the process of writing this book. You guys are amazing.

To all of my many friends, without whom life would be boring. Especially Victoria, for believing in me from the start and always helping me. My lifelong friends Catherine, Donna, Sam and Steph, who have always supported me and those that have encouraged me, especially Ruth & Dalj, Alison & Nick, Paul & Lisa, Margaret, Pam, and Dot and also my new friends Morgan Grace, Toni, Alex, Martyn, Elle and Hollie.

To my inspiring charcuterie community from across the pond in the USA, especially my friends Kelsey and Jen, Mo, Carly, Amanda, Cynthia, Olivia, Ashley, and Alison who have all inspired me and will continue to do so with their wonderful cheese creations.

To the people who have helped to bring out my creativity through various projects. Each time these businesses and colleagues have asked me to create something, it expanded my knowledge and brought me closer to where I am now. Drew, Heidi, Laura & James, Kim, Lauren, Seema, Dee, and Steph, thank you for trusting me. Finally, some of my favourite suppliers: Simon, Zoe, Sophie, Ric, Chole (Unify PR) and Diana (Viners).

There are many more and will continue to be more people who help make this creative cheese journey of mine one that I will never, ever forget. To everyone who has helped me in one way or another, family, friend, business colleague, client or reader, I cannot thank you enough.

WHAT OR WHO INSPIRES YOU?
WHAT MOTIVATES YOU IN LIFE?

Inspiration is everywhere: a song on the radio, trees and flowers, a slow sunset, a friend's caring words, a good book, the love we give and receive, happy memories and trying new experiences. Food has the most amazing way of transporting us to another place: the smells, tastes and textures often make us reminisce about happy times. I hope that this book will inspire you to reflect on a happy time, place or experience and create something special.

For me, one of the biggest inspirations is nature: the colours, changing seasons, endless varieties of fruit and vegetables… I love to grow my own fruit and veg and spend time outside in nature, around the trees and flowers, taking inspiration from them and creating something from that.

Over the past few years, my interest in food, particularly in cheese and its authenticity, has really grown. I love all things local, and by utilising your local businesses to buy cheeses and other produce, you are helping them, the local economy and the environment. Produce from the farms in your area will also taste better because it's bound to be fresher. My local farm grows the most amazing variety of berries and vegetables, which I adore when they are in season.

I hope that you find pleasure in creating the recipes in this book, but also use your creativity to inspire your own grazing. Use this book to assist you in creating graze boards that reflect your personality, your loves and your passions in life. You can take little bits from the recipes that you like and make them your own, whether that's a taste, colour, a particular theme or even a particular cheese.

I want you to read this book and be as passionate about preparing a cheeseboard as I am. They can be beautiful works of art that are not only delicious to eat, but a relaxing pastime to make. It's a great way to escape the daily grind. There are no rules for creating a cheeseboard or grazing platter; if you love the elements that are on there - the flavours, textures and combinations - then that's all that matters. Your cheeseboard is an amazing cheeseboard.

If you want to swap something out or leave something off a board, that's fine. This book is simply your starting point. I'll give you some of my favourite combinations with plenty of hints and tips along the way, but the most important thing is to have fun, share, taste and enjoy. There is nothing more rewarding than presenting a plate of food that you have prepared for your favourite people to share, and seeing the looks of joy on their faces as they admire your creation.

I'd love this book to be your destination when you need to unwind, when you need a quick fix for dinner or want to entertain, or just because you need some comfort food and feel like getting creative. Be inspired: not only by this book, but by the world we live in and the things that bring you joy, then have fun making your own beautiful creations.

HOW TO BEGIN:
BOARDS, PLATES & TRAYS

The starting point to any grazing board is the platter or board itself. You can use plates, slates, chopping boards or trays. Wood, ceramic, slate and marble are all good materials that will last and look beautiful. I think that no matter what you put on a board or platter, it automatically elevates your meal, whether that's beans on toast or the most elaborate cheeseboard, it just looks good. Don't you agree?

When deciding what to arrange your cheeseboard on, this is entirely a personal choice. From a beautiful antique tray to a contemporary serving plate or your Granny's old chopping board, the platter will set the tone and feel of your occasion. Where appropriate, I have suggested sizes and types in my recipes, but of course this also depends on what you have available. Collecting platters, boards and serving trays is another of my hobbies! I regularly sneak them into the house so my husband doesn't see my ever-expanding collection…

Wooden boards are my favourite and come in an array of shapes and sizes. Make sure they are food-safe by following all the necessary guidance depending on the type of wood and the finish. For striking presentation, a good rule of thumb is to go for a lighter coloured wood if you are serving darker foods, and vice versa. These are perfect for creating a 'rustic chic' look, whereas marble lends itself to classy and elegant cheeseboards. Choose neutral colours for everyday boards and vibrant or unusual platters for special occasions. Kitsch and vintage items can add a fun retro factor to your creations. Stone and slate keeps your food cold, and trays with edges are always a good choice for keeping your food in place.

UTENSILS & STORAGE

It's so important to have good quality kitchen utensils when preparing your ingredients. Good knives and chopping boards are almost as important as the presentation board itself. I would recommend purchasing the best quality knives you can afford. I have been a loyal customer of Viners for years; they are an iconic British company and the quality and aesthetics of their products are outstanding. I also recommend OXO for items that you will need in this book such as scissors, kitchen scales, a salad spinner and a good quality mandoline for thinly slicing fruits, vegetables and cheeses.

You will also need good quality storage jars for many of the recipes in this book. Kilner jars are a firm favourite with me and have been for years; mine still look just as new as the day I purchased them. Again, it's so worth investing in the best kitchenware you can afford.

CROCKERY & CUTLERY

Vintage cheese knives and decorative spoons add to the drama and feel of your boards. Ramekins (small wooden, glass or metal bowls) are ideal for liquid or wet foods such as hummus, olives and dips. I prefer glass or white ceramic ramekins as they really stand out on your boards. Alternatively, use disposable tubs for ease when cleaning up. You can also use linen and napkins to elevate the mood further and make sure things don't get too messy for your guests.

WHERE TO FIND
THE BEST PRODUCE

I like to shop at my local farm shop, Kenyon Hall Farm, which is five minutes from my home. In the summer, as well as using my own homegrown products, I love to go strawberry and raspberry picking with the family. We always get carried away, buy more than we need, and then make some amazing jam to enjoy all year round.

I am very lucky to have some beautiful farms and artisan food shops where I live, such as The Cheshire Smokehouse in Wilmslow which is one of my top spots for picking up local, seasonal, fresh produce. The Cheese Yard in Knutsford is home to my local cheesemonger, where I love to try brand new cheeses and have long conversations all about cheese! There's also a brilliant greengrocers which I call my Aladdin's cave; I always buy lots of produce there and chat to the staff about what's in season. The Hollies Farm Shop in Little Budworth and Bents Garden Centre in Glazebury, which has a fantastic food hall, are more local favourites.

I also love to shop at my regional supermarket, Booths. Here I can find an array of unusual items for my boards that aren't readily available in the bigger supermarkets. Don't get me wrong, I like to shop in the national chains too, but I would urge you to start with small businesses first, as this is where the good stuff can always be found. Look up your nearest bee farmer and investigate whether you can buy honeycomb from them; my local is Bax Bees and I've really never tasted anything like their honey: it's divine. Have fun finding your local farms and dairies, and ask your neighbours whether they grow or make anything that could enhance your boards in exchange for some homemade goodies!

CHOOSING CHEESES

Buying local cheese is a wonderful way to support your community and inject money back into the local economy. By visiting the nearest farm shop, buying from your cheesemonger or making a conscious decision to buy more of your everyday items from producers in the area, you really do make a difference to small businesses and to the environment. In Cheshire there are a number of cheese producers including Hayfields Dairy, The Cheshire Cheese Company, Orsom Cheese and Joseph Heeler.

Have fun researching the specialty cheeses that are on your doorstep. I can spend hours reading about cheese making and learning about the UK's amazing producers. Whole books are dedicated to these subjects, so I won't attempt to summarise them here. I'll only say see what's out there, try a new cheese every month as a treat, and what's the harm if you don't like it? You may even find your new favourite!

When it comes to serving your cheeses, always let them come to room temperature before eating and make the accompaniments special. Seasonal fruits, local honey and anything you can grow yourself will reward you with amazing flavours. As the saying goes, what grows together, goes together. For more specialist boards, naturally local produce is not always possible, but you can still seek out the best, such as Maters & Co for small batch specialist honey.

Your cheese is going to take center stage when it comes to most of the boards and platters in this book, so by choosing an array of textures and tastes, you will be adding more depth and interest to your creation. I generally like to include a good cheddar because it's very versatile and most people like it. Always try to put a minimum of two or three cheeses on your boards that either complement or contrast each other.

CHEESE TEXTURES

The main types of cheese are broken down into the following categories by their texture:

FRESH. Serve fresh cheeses like burrata and mozzarella in ramekins or bowls because they are fairly wet. Other examples are cream cheese, ricotta, mascarpone and cottage cheese.

SOFT & BLOOMY. Cheeses like brie, feta and Kidderton Ash goat's cheese are creamy in texture. These cheeses pair well with sweet honey and figs.

WASHED RIND. These are mainly 'stinky' cheeses, which aren't to everyone's taste and so you won't find many recipes within the book containing them. They are generally recognised by their orange rinds and include cheeses such as Époisses, Muenster, Taleggio and our own famous Stinking Bishop.

SEMI-SOFT. These cheeses pair well with dark breads like rye and pumpernickel. Examples include Cornish yarg and fontina.

HARD. A hard cheese is the best for cutting and slicing, such as mature cheddar, Red Leicester, Lancashire, Manchego and parmesan.

BLUE. This category pairs well with sweet compotes, jams and dips. Examples include Stilton, Blacksticks Blue, gorgonzola, Roquefort and Danish Blue. You'll also see that some blue cheeses are in fact green. Many people say they don't like blue cheese; I was one of them until recently and all I can say is try Montagnolo Affine. It's a soft and creamy German blue cheese that has won awards and you never know, you may be converted!

Cheese can also be made with a variety of different milks, from the most commonly used cow's milk to sheep's milk, goat's milk and even buffalo milk.

HOW TO CUT &
ARRANGE YOUR CHEESE

Cheeses can be bought and cut in a variety of shapes and sizes, including blocks, large or small wheels, wedges, logs, cones and bite-size cubes. The drawings opposite should help to illustrate this.

You will see the various ways I like to cut and arrange cheese in the photographs throughout this book. The techniques I use most often are:

A neat stack of cheese cubes or triangles. See page 110 for an example.

A rosette, where I cut a brie-style cheese into small wedges and arrange them around a ramekin to create a rosette shape. See page 66 for an example.

A zig zag or 'zip' pattern, where I cut harder cheeses such as Manchego, Red Leicester or cheddar into triangles and arrange them in alternating directions. I usually use six slices of cheese for this. See page 74 for an example.

A shell or fan, where long thin triangles are arranged in a seashell or fan shape. See page 84 for an example.

A tornado, where cheese slices are laid on top of each other to form a funnel shape.

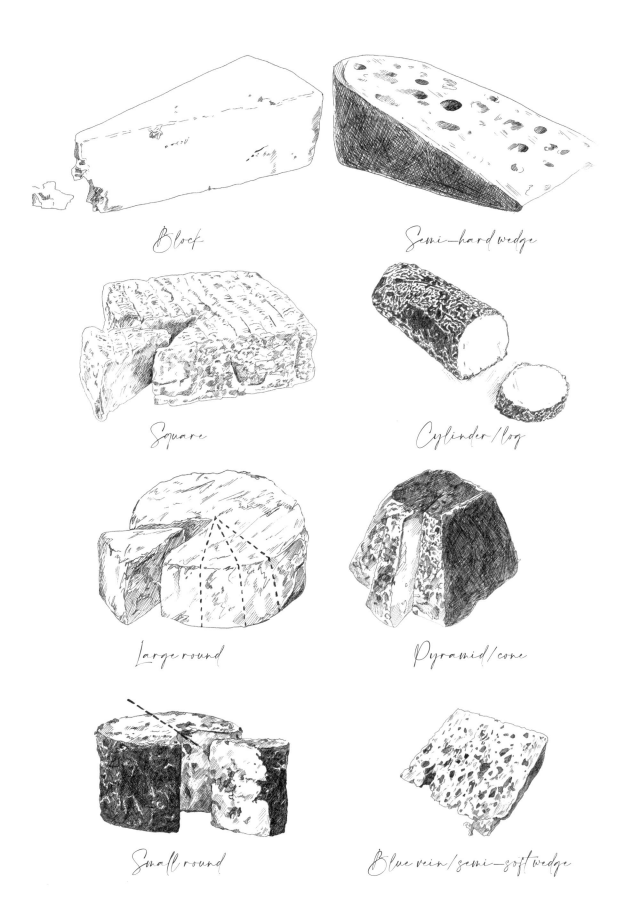

Block

Semi-hard wedge

Square

Cylinder/log

Large round

Pyramid/cone

Small round

Blue vein/semi-soft wedge

SERVINGS & ACCOMPANIMENTS

SERVINGS

As a rule of thumb, you should be serving around 125 to 150g of cheese and meats per guest for a main meal. Reduce this to between 65 and 85g if serving your cheeseboard as an after dinner treat or snack.

MEATS

The best meats for cheeseboards are charcuterie (dried meats) as they can be left out for longer periods of time. My favourite meats to add are salami, saucisson and bresaola, but pâté, speck and coppa or even smoked fish would also work well.

CARBS

All good grazing boards need a carbohydrate, and which one you choose is entirely up to you. Naturally, some will work better than others depending on the contents of your board. Wheat crackers, pretzels, toasts, baguettes, pitta breads, water biscuits, crostini, focaccia, breadsticks, pumpernickel and tiger bread are just a few of the options here.

PICKLES

Olives and other pickled or marinated foods help to cleanse the palate between each bite. Why not try pickled carrots, peppers and even sprouts? Cranberries also pickle really well too… in fact, you can pickle just about any fruit or veg you like!

FRESH FRUIT

Grapes and figs are an essential part of most cheeseboards, but consider the different cheeses that you are using to find the perfect pairing. Another whole book could be written on these pairings, but I have tried to give you some ideas within the recipes of fruits and cheeses that work well together. Apples and pears work well with many cheeses, and berries generally complement softer cheeses.

DRIED FRUIT & NUTS

Salted or candied nuts such as almonds, pecans and walnuts will enhance any board. Try making your own and play with the flavours. Dried apricots, apple slices and cranberries are all great accompaniments to a grazing board too.

SWEET TREATS

Consider adding shards of good quality chocolate, homemade chocolate bark or sweet candied nuts to your boards. The combination of salty and sweet is delicious, so don't be afraid to mix it up even if you're not making a dessert board.

CONDIMENTS

The possibilities here are endless; delicatessens, farm shops and specialists are packed with beautiful chutneys, jams, preserves and honey. Sample these if you can, or have a go at making your own with the recipes in this book. Aioli and mustards add flavour, interest and contrast to your boards too. My favourite chutneys are made by The Cherry Tree, Mrs. Darlington's and Tiptree.

GARNISHES

The garnish is one of my favourite parts of creating any graze board. It's where you can really have fun, personalising by theme, colour and season. Try decorating your boards with edible flowers, herbs such as rosemary and oregano, stems of waxflowers and chrysanthemums, pine cones and dried orange slices around Christmas time, and seasonal treats such as love heart chocolates for Valentine's Day.

PERFECT PAIRINGS

Here are a few examples of some excellent pairings, but remember: if you love it, that's all that matters.

Brie and apples (this is a match made in heaven!)

Smoked Gouda or gorgonzola and figs

Camembert with almonds, apples and pears

Gouda with apples, grapes, olives and pears

Manchego with apples, almonds, and pears

Époisses and peaches

Brie with walnuts and honey

Ricotta or Stilton and cherries

Parmesan and sun-dried tomatoes

Spring

INSPIRATION IS EVERYWHERE:
A SONG ON THE RADIO, TREES AND FLOWERS, A SLOW SUNSET,
A FRIEND'S CARING WORDS, A GOOD BOOK, THE LOVE WE GIVE
AND RECEIVE, HAPPY MEMORIES AND TRYING NEW EXPERIENCES.

The Grasmere board

The picturesque village of Grasmere inspired me to make this board; I love walking and spending time in the Lake District. In the words of William Wordsworth, Grasmere is 'the loveliest spot that man hath ever found' and green is in abundance both there and on this board.

ingredients

250g green grapes

200g olives

1 Boursin

2 sticks of celery

1½ pears

200g blue cheese

1 small jar of caramelised onion chutney (see recipe on page 162)

1 Romanesco broccoli

100g mangetout and sugar snap peas

3 asparagus spears

2 spring onions

1 green apple

1 packet of Heart & Flour Almond and Pecan Toast (or your favourite crackers)

2 kiwi fruits

15g pistachios

Handful of cress, to garnish

Basil or other soft herbs, to garnish

method

Take a round board or tray that is approximately 35cm in diameter. Put the grapes and olives into separate ramekins or small bowls and place these on your board.

Unwrap the Boursin, just peeling back the edges so the cheese is still sitting in the wrapper, and place it on your board. Alternatively, take off all the wrapping and place the cheese in another ramekin.

Wash the celery then slice the sticks into thin strips and arrange on your board. Cut the pears lengthways into quarters and place next to the celery.

Cut or crumble the blue cheese into large chunks and arrange them on the board. Place the small jar of chutney on the board with a teaspoon.

Leave the Romanesco broccoli whole and sit this next to the other greens. When everyone sits down to eat, they can cut chunks off to eat with the Boursin.

Stand the mangetout and sugar snap peas upright in a short glass or ramekin and place this on your board. Fill in any spaces with the asparagus and spring onion, then slice the apple horizontally and stack it back together on the board.

Arrange the toasts or crackers on the board in a neat line around the edge. Slice the kiwi fruits, removing the skin first if preferred, and place in the remaining gaps.

Finally, add the pistachios in a neat pile and garnish the board with cress, basil and any other herbs of your choice. Your board is now ready to serve.

pair with...

A cloudy apple juice, a pear cocktail with gin or a dry white wine would pair beautifully with this crisp, green board.

The Amalfi board

This board has been inspired by my love of Italy. Cannoli are sweet Sicilian pastries, and this 'build your own' style board is sure to be a hit. You can play around with the flavours of the dip and add your own favourites, such as lemon and raspberry.

ingredients

150g fudge pieces

150g pistachios

150g white chocolate chips

150g dark chocolate chips

250g milk chocolate chips

200g biscotti

150g Wright & Co. Brandy Snaps

For the cannoli whip

300g ricotta

250g mascarpone

250g icing sugar

¾ tsp vanilla extract

¾ tsp almond extract

method

Start by making the whip. Combine all the ingredients in a food processor and blend for around 5 minutes until thick and creamy. Decant the mixture into a pretty bowl for serving.

Find a bowl with individual sections or several smaller bowls, and fill with the fudge, pistachios and chocolate chips, reserving 100g of the milk chocolate chips for melting.

Stack the biscotti and brandy snaps on a cake stand alongside the whip. Just before serving, crush some of the pistachios and melt the remaining milk chocolate chips for drizzling over the biscuits.

Build your own 'cannoli' and enjoy! For an extra taste of Amalfi, add 1 to 2 tablespoons of lemon juice to your whip instead of the almond extract, and decorate the bowl with fresh raspberries.

pair with... Go for a limoncello, martini or amaretto for a truly Italian after-dinner experience!

The Lancashire board

They say home is where the heart is, and my home county of Lancashire will always make me proud to be a Northerner. Lancashire is renowned for its beautiful countryside, cheerful locals and world-famous cheeses. This rustic board uses some from Lancashire's most famous producers.

ingredients

400g black grapes

150g blackberries

100g strawberries

100g redcurrants

75g cherries

80g smoked nuts (such as almonds)

100g Miller's Plum & Date Toast

150g Kidderton Ash goat's cheese

50g Mrs Butler's Lancashire cheese

120g Bowland Lancashire cheese

70g Button Mill soft cheese

1 apple

1 pear

method

I have used a marble paddle board approximately 17cm in diameter to make the colours stand out, but any board of roughly the same size (or 30cm in length if rectangular) will work here. Use a small cake stand or serving plate for the grapes, berries, redcurrants and cherries.

Place the nuts in a small ramekin or bowl on your board. Arrange the plum and date toasts in a neat stack. Slice the goat's cheese into rounds and arrange in a neat line on your board.

Slice the Lancashire cheese into long thin strips, cut the Bowland Lancashire into triangles and quarter the Button Mill, then cut the quarters in half again. Arrange all the cheeses on your board.

Place the apple and pear, left whole or sliced as preferred, on your board and serve it with some locally produced onion chutney.

pair with... Lancashire is full of breweries and gin distilleries. Pick your favourite local beer, pour yourself a gin and tonic, or - as Lancashire is home to one of Britain's last original temperance bars - opt for a traditional soft drink such as dandelion and burdock or cream soda.

The Little Graze board

I love to have cheese and crackers for my lunch, as a snack in the evening or sometimes in place of a large dinner. This is my go-to cheeseboard for those occasions. It's simple but tasty and includes all my favourite bites.

ingredients

85g mature cheddar

25g walnuts

50g petit brie cheese

45g Miller's Plum & Date Toast

85g red seedless grapes

30g dried apricots

½ a pear

Local honey and caramelised onion chutney (see recipe on page 162)

method

Start by cutting the cheddar into triangles and arranging them on a small board that is roughly 20cm by 15cm. Fill a small ramekin with walnuts and place on your board.

Cut the brie into triangles and arrange around the ramekin of walnuts. Neatly stack the toasts on the board and put the grapes in a pile next to them. Add the dried apricots.

Thinly slice the pear and arrange on your board. Serve with fresh local honey and your favourite cheeseboard chutney.

My favourite bites on this board are brie, honey and walnut or mature cheddar with a quality caramelised onion chutney, which is just divine!

pair with... As this is my favourite board, anything goes. I like a raspberry gin or sometimes a rosé wine with it, but if I'm having this board at lunchtime I love a cloudy apple juice or cup of Yorkshire tea with my cheeseboard.

The Chocolate Eggs for breakfast board

Easter morning always brings back memories of chocolate eggs for breakfast. This is a fun board for adults and children alike with a French twist. Drizzle the honey onto the cheese and finish with the elegant macarons. Add more of your favourite cheese or flowers for a spectacular spring display.

ingredients

30g mini chocolate eggs

250g mini foil-wrapped Easter eggs

10 macarons

115g Comté

100g Buchette Chevre aux Miel et Fleurs (goat's cheese with honey and dried flowers, or any other soft cheese)

200g red grapes

3 apricots

1 packet of sourdough flatbreads

½ a fresh orange

5 slices of dried orange (see recipe on page 182)

28g pot of French honey (or any honey of your choice)

Butter, apricot jam and croissants, to serve

method

Find a board that is approximately 30cm in diameter. Put the mini eggs and foil-wrapped chocolates into separate ramekins and place them on your board. Arrange the macarons around the edge of the ramekins.

Slice the Comté into triangles and arrange them in alternate directions on your board. Place the goat's cheese log in the centre.

Pile the grapes neatly to one side and place the apricots next to them. Lay the flatbreads in the corner of the board at an angle.

Garnish your board with the fresh and dried orange then serve it with the pot of honey, butter, jam and warm croissants.

pair with... This breakfast board pairs well with raspberry or other fruit teas. For a full on chocolate fix, why not try hot chocolate with cream!

The Gioiosa Caprese board

One of my favourite salads is the classic caprese: simple, elegant and tasty. With the colours of the Italian flag, and elements of antipasto, this board is as versatile as you want it to be. Perfect for late spring lunches with friends in the garden.

ingredients

80g parmesan

1 galia melon

1 cantaloupe melon

2 tbsp balsamic vinegar

2 tbsp pesto

75g gorgonzola

6 slices of Parma ham

1 ball of mozzarella

1 large tomato

100g Milano salami

3 asparagus spears

1 head of chicory

1 fig

2 apricots

5 yellow cherry tomatoes

Fresh basil and oregano, to garnish

200g sun-dried tomatoes

200g olives

100g pine nuts

method

First, grate the parmesan and scoop it onto a non-stick baking sheet in mounds of 2 or 3 tablespoons. Season with salt and pepper, then bake the parmesan in a moderately hot oven for approximately 18 to 20 minutes until melted and golden brown. Allow the parmesan crisps to cool on the tray before removing them carefully with a palette knife.

Take a board or tray that is approximately 35cm by 25cm and place the parmesan crisps on one side of it. Halve the galia melon and scoop out spheres of the flesh using a melon baller. Place these in a small bowl and set that in the centre of your board. Cut three slices from the cantaloupe melon.

Measure the balsamic vinegar and pesto into separate small ramekins and place them on your board.

Place the gorgonzola next to the bowl of melon.

Roll half of the Parma ham slices into cylinders and place them between the slices of cantaloupe on the board. Cut the mozzarella and the tomato into slices of an even thickness and alternate these on your board, with each one slightly overlapping the next.

Slice the salami and overlap the discs in a line next to the mozzarella and tomato. Blanch the asparagus by bringing a pan of water to the boil and dropping the spears in to cook for 2 to 3 minutes. Using a slotted spoon, transfer the asparagus straight to a bowl of iced water. Once cool, dry the spears then wrap them individually in the remaining slices of Parma ham. Arrange these on your board.

Separate the chicory into individual leaves and arrange them on your board. Halve the fig and place next to the chicory, add the apricots and cherry tomatoes, then garnish with basil and oregano.

If you like, fill additional ramekins with the sun-dried tomatoes, olives and pine nuts for an extra bite to eat. Serve your board with breadsticks, focaccia or crusty bread on the side.

pair with... A pinot grigio, pinot bianco, your favourite rosé wine or a rosé margarita cocktail would be a great accompaniment here. For a non-alcoholic drink, go for a pink lemonade.

The Ma Chérie board

Paris is world-renowned for being the city of love; a romantic break in the French capital wouldn't be complete without a little fromage, eaten on the cobbled streets outside a café while watching the world go by. I was inspired to create this particular board by a trip to the beautiful Sacré-Cœur Basilica in Montmartre.

ingredients

200g Neufchâtel cheese (or brie, if unavailable)

45g Maroilles (a semi-soft washed rind cheese)

25g Crottin de Chavignol goat's cheese

25g Saint Nectaire (a semi-soft washed rind cheese)

25g Fourme d'Ambert (a semi-hard blue cheese)

Selection of seasonal red berries

1 fig, halved

75g beetroot or sea salted crackers

65g seedless red grapes

30g Tatton trail mix (see recipe on page 178)

30g white chocolate, rose petal and pistachio bark (see recipe on page 186)

Redcurrants and fresh mint, to garnish

method

Place the Neufchâtel two thirds of the way down a board that is approximately 32cm by 17cm. Leave the cheese whole, or cut as per the instructions on page 18.

Place the Maroilles, Crottin de Chavignol, Saint Nectaire and Fourme d'Ambert on your board. Arrange the selection of seasonal berries neatly in the corner of your board. Place the fig halves between the cheeses, and lay the crackers in a curved overlapping line at the bottom corner of your board. Pile the grapes next to them.

Lay the Tatton trail mix and white chocolate bark in the remaining spaces on the board, and then garnish with the redcurrants and fresh mint.

Serve with a good quality French chestnut honey, or any honey of your choice.

pair with... No French cheeseboard would be complete without a glass of champagne — my favourite being Veuve Clicquot — or a refreshing French pilsner.

The Portofino board

Cobbled streets, fishing boats, sipping wine, chatting with friends and dining al fresco all remind me of beautiful Portofino in Italy. This board takes me back to a summer almost 20 years ago when I first tasted burrata there. The colours remind me of the vibrant painted buildings that line the harbour.

ingredients

125g burrata

2 tbsp olive oil

2 tsp pesto

2 nectarines

Handful of rocket

6-10 cherry or baby plum tomatoes

1 ledicia or heirloom tomato

1 packet of bruschetta toasts or crostini

10 cherries

30g candied pecans (see recipe on page 176)

1 fig

2 radishes

2 apricots

1 red pepper

6 sprigs of oregano, to garnish

1 lemon, quartered

Balsamic glaze

Salt and pepper

Focaccia, to serve (optional)

method

Place the burrata carefully in a ramekin or shallow bowl and pour the olive oil over the top. Place the ramekin on a circular board or tray that is approximately 30cm in diameter. Decant the pesto into a smaller ramekin and add this to your board.

Slice the nectarines and remove the stones, then arrange the fruit around the burrata bowl. Pile the rocket next to the bowl.

Halve the cherry tomatoes, slice the ledicia or heirloom tomato and arrange them all on your board. Arrange the toasts or crostini along one edge and pile the cherries next to them.

Put the candied pecans into a small ramekin or bowl and place on your board. Halve or quarter the fig and radishes, then place these into the gaps along with the whole apricots.

Deseed the red pepper, slice into strips and arrange these on your board. Garnish with the oregano and a wedge of lemon, then drizzle some balsamic glaze over the large sliced tomato.

Finally, season your burrata with salt and pepper and place a small sprig of oregano on top. Serve the board with focaccia on the side instead of bruschetta toasts or crostini if you like.

pair with...

Enjoy this board with a bottle of your favourite sauvignon blanc, pinot noir or an Aperol spritz.

The Smörgåsbord

This Scandinavian-style board will transport you to Sweden. It's perfect for making ahead, leaving you free to entertain guests, but also works well as a family dinner. This board would be even more fun with some Scandipop playing in the background like ABBA or a-ha!

ingredients

85g Tine Gudbrandsdalen Brunost (Norwegian brown cheese)

150g candied pecans (see recipe on page 176)

135g Jarlsberg cheese

1 small pear

115g green grapes

50g Peter's Yard Original Sourdough Crackers

For the mackerel pâté

250g smoked mackerel

200g cream cheese

1 tbsp capers

½ lemon, juiced

Large handful of fresh dill, chopped

Sea salt and black pepper

For the cucumber salad

1 whole cucumber

100ml white vinegar

1 tsp each of salt and sugar

For the hasselback potatoes

175g new potatoes

Olive oil

method

For the mackerel pâté

Combine the mackerel, cream cheese, capers, lemon juice and most of the fresh dill in a food processor, then season to taste with salt and pepper. Blend to your preferred consistency, then decant the pâté into a small ramekin or bowl and garnish with a sprig of dill and a slice of lemon.

For the cucumber salad

Using a vegetable peeler or mandoline, peel the cucumber lengthways to make long 'ribbons'. Place these in a bowl and add 75ml of the vinegar with 50ml of water and the salt and sugar. Leave the cucumber to marinate for 5 minutes, then pour off two thirds of the liquid. Gradually add the remaining vinegar and a sprinkle of salt to taste, then toss to mix everything. Arrange the cucumber salad in a serving bowl and scatter some chopped dill over the top.

For the hasselback potatoes

Slice each new potato almost but not quite all the way through several times, working along the length from one end to the other. Brush them thoroughly with olive oil and cook in a preheated oven at 180°c for around 30 minutes, or until golden and crispy. Remove the hasselback potatoes from the oven when they are cooked, then leave to cool slightly before sprinkling with sea salt to serve.

Place your bowls of mackerel pâté, cucumber salad and hasselback potatoes on a circular board around 35cm in diameter. Cut the Norwegian brown cheese into cubes and place in another bowl on the board. Fill a ramekin with the candied pecans and add this to the board. Slice the Jarlsberg and arrange in a fan on your board, then do the same with the pear. Arrange the grapes and crackers in neat stacks, then garnish with any remaining dill. You could also add the simple salad on page 152 to this board.

pair with...

Take your pick from either a glass of Linie Aquavit, a traditional Norwegian potato-based spirit, or Voss bottled water for a cool, refreshing Nordic hit.

The Rustic French board

Understated elegance always takes me back to the cobbled streets of Paris. This rustic cheeseboard, with French simplicity as its inspiration, makes me think of winter breaks wandering through the beautiful capital city, eating warm baguettes with the most amazing cheese.

ingredients

80g Roquefort

50g French blue cheese

50g Ossau-Iraty (sheep's milk cheese)

50g Doux de Montagne (traditional cow's milk cheese)

75g saucisson sec

90g black grapes

6 physalis

2 fresh figs

15g blackberries

1 baguette, to serve

French honey (optional)

method

Simply cut the cheeses into wedges and arrange them in a line on the long side of a 30cm by 17cm board, placing each one at an angle with the triangles pointing in the same direction.

Slice the saucisson sec and arrange in a neat stack on your board. Place the grapes next to the saucisson, and the physalis next to the grapes. Quarter the figs and arrange them with the blackberries in the corner of your board. Serve with the baguette and French honey, if using.

pair with... A Bordeaux or red wine from the Rhône would marry well with this board, as would a tawny Port.

The Spring Garland

This feta and watermelon salad is perfect as a standalone dish, or an accompaniment to the other boards within the book. The muted spring tones and fresh ingredients make it a great choice for long, lazy bank holiday weekends.

ingredients

60g pea shoots

50g radishes

100g watermelon

20g sugar snap peas

50g cucumber

100g feta cheese

Cress, to garnish

method

You will need a paddle board approximately 30cm in diameter. Start by placing the pea shoots around the edge of the board to create a ring.

Next, thinly slice the radishes and arrange them over the pea shoots. Cut the watermelon into bite-size cubes and distribute these evenly all around the wreath shape you are creating.

Slice the sugar snap peas open down one long side, so you can see the peas inside, then add them to your board. Dice the cucumber and arrange the pieces on the garland.

Finally, cut the feta into small cubes and space them around the ring, then garnish the board with cress or spring flowers before serving with a simple salad dressing of your choice.

pair with... This simple salad is refreshing and light, so a rosé wine or simple cocktail would pair well with it.

The Philly Cheesesteak Slider board

The USA is one of my favourite holiday destinations. Alongside a classic American cheeseburger, the Philly cheesesteak sandwich is one of my go-to fast food treats when I visit. The gooey melted cheese, charred steak and moist onion and peppers are just a match made in heaven.

ingredients

150g frying steak

1 red onion

1 red pepper

1 yellow pepper

80g baby sweetcorn

80g baby cucumber

½ a tomato

6 mini slider buns

50g provolone, sliced

15g rocket

method

Start by cutting the steak into thin strips and dicing the onion and peppers into small cubes. Add the steak, onion, pepper and baby sweetcorn to a medium-hot frying pan and cook for 5 to 6 minutes, until softened and just beginning to char. Meanwhile, slice the cucumber and tomato.

Line the bottom half of each bun with slices of provolone and place them in a row on a board measuring approximately 35cm by 15cm. Arrange the cucumber and tomato on the board, then add the steak, onion, peppers and sweetcorn when they are cooked. You might want to use a small bowl to hold the diced vegetables. Lastly, place the rocket on your board.

Pile your chosen fillings into a slider bun while the steak and vegetables are still hot, allowing the cheese to melt. Season with a pinch of salt to taste before tucking in.

pair with... Pick up a Coca-Cola, Pepsi or Budweiser for a refreshing carbonated treat alongside your mini cheesesteak burgers.

The Beaumaris board

The thought of Wales just fills my heart with joy. Childhood holidays, stunning beaches, castles steeped in history and the warmth of the people make it a place that everyone should visit. The Welsh are also really good at making cheese and this board contains some of my favourites.

ingredients

100g Caws Teifi Traditional Caerphilly cheese

100g Snowdonia Black Bomber (Welsh cheddar cheese)

100g Perl Wen (Welsh soft cheese)

2 fresh figs

30g green grapes

30g red seedless grapes

80g Cradoc's Pear and Earl Grey Savoury Biscuits

Handful of smoked nuts of your choice

Dylan's Fruit Chutney, to serve

method

Cut the Caws Teifi cheese into triangles and arrange on a board that is approximately 30cm by 17cm in diameter.

Remove the Snowdonia cheddar from its wax coating, and cut the cheese in half. Reserve one half for another day. Cut the remaining piece of cheese into eighths and arrange in a neat stack on your board.

Do the same with the Perl Wen cheese. Note this is a runny cheese and will need to be served straight from the fridge in order to stay firm enough for slicing.

Halve the figs and place them on your board, then arrange the grapes in bunches of 3 or 4 around the cheeses.

Place the crackers in a corner of the board, pop the nuts into a ramekin and then serve your board alongside the fruit chutney.

pair with… A real Welsh ale, such as Cwtch from the Tiny Rebel brewery, would complement this board very well, as would a sparkling white wine or a red produced in Wales at the White Castle Vineyard.

The Spring Salad

These spring vegetables are fresh and light, making a salad that works on its own or as an accompaniment to your spring graze boards. It's simple and easy to make; just swap out any of the ingredients you don't like, add some grilled chicken for a protein-rich option or keep it meat-free with feta or parmesan.

ingredients

1 white cabbage

2 red onions

125g radishes

150g sugar snap peas

1 yellow pepper

1 punnet of cress

Sea salt (optional)

Simple salad dressing (see recipe on page 156)

method

Finely slice the white cabbage, red onions and radishes into a large bowl using a mandoline. If you don't have a mandoline, simply cut the vegetables as thinly as possible with a sharp knife.

Cut the sugar snap peas into bite-size pieces and pop them into the bowl. Deseed the yellow pepper, then dice into small cubes and add them to your bowl along with the cress.

Toss the salad until everything is evenly distributed, season with salt if you like and then serve with a simple salad dressing of your choice.

pair with... Lots of drinks will complement the clean flavours of this salad, so simply choose a crisp white wine, local lager or soft drink of your choice.

Summer

FOOD HAS THE MOST AMAZING WAY OF TRANSPORTING US TO ANOTHER PLACE: THE SMELLS, TASTES AND TEXTURES OFTEN MAKE US REMINISCE ABOUT HAPPY TIMES.

The Rainbow board

This board pays homage to music, art, poetry, creativity, love, light and positivity. The rainbow has been a symbol of hope for centuries. "Rainbows introduce us to reflections of different beautiful possibilities so we never forget that pain and grief are not the final options in life." ~ Aberjhani

ingredients

160g raspberries

150g black grapes

200g red grapes

180g green grapes

75g physalis

80g strawberries

45g blackcurrants

45g blackberries

115g cherries

40g redcurrants

45g blueberries

For the fruit dip

330ml double cream

250ml mascarpone cheese

2 tbsp icing sugar

4 cherries, stoned

4 blackberries

4 raspberries

4 strawberries

4 blueberries

method

A circular board approximately 35cm in diameter with a raised edge is best for this display. Place the raspberries in two rows around the edge of half the board. You could use them in different ways to add interest, such as alternating the direction they face.

Halve the black grapes and arrange them on the opposite side of the board, so they almost meet the raspberries at the edges. Fill in any gaps between the raspberries and black grapes with some of the other grapes and physalis, so that you have a full outer circle of fruit.

Slice the strawberries into quarters and place them on your board inside the semicircle of raspberries. Place the blackcurrants on your board inside the semicircle of black grapes, then fill the rest of that row with the blackberries.

Add a row of cherries next to the strawberries and fill any gaps with the redcurrants. Place the blueberries next to the blackberries and you should be left with a small gap between the two sides.

Fill this space with the remaining red grapes, then the green grapes and physalis, overlapping the colours to create interest and contrast.

To make the fruit dip, combine all the ingredients in a food processor or blender. Decant the dip into a ramekin or small bowl and serve alongside your board.

pair with... A freshly squeezed fruit juice, ice-cold infused water or herbal/fruit tea would complement this board beautifully.

The British Rustic Chic board

Home interiors are one of my absolute passions in life. For many years, I have been inspired by one designer in particular. Her designs are elegant, classy and her style is perfect in every way. I have chosen the best British cheeses to reflect this, with neutral tones to reflect the colour palette of the interiors I love so much.

ingredients

250g King Stone Dairy Rollright (washed rind soft cheese)

200g Neal's Yard Dairy Ragstone (mature goat's cheese)

200g Brinkworth Dairy Royal Bassett Blue

200g Tor (soft goat's milk cheese)

200g Ashlynn Goat's Cheese

200g Clara Goat's Cheese

125g Mature Blue Stilton

100g Finn (handmade soft cheese)

100g your favourite mature cheddar

1 packet of Peter's Yard Rye & Charcoal Sourdough Crackers

1 packet of Peter's Yard Original Sourdough Crackers

100g seedless red grapes

Handful of physalis, to garnish

150g candied pecans (see recipe on page 176)

Quality local honey or honeycomb, to serve

method

You will need a board measuring roughly 30cm by 17cm and a small cake stand to add contrast and height to your creation.

Simply cut the cheeses according to the guide on page 18 and then arrange them on the board and cake stand. This really is something you can have fun with. I have chosen cheeses that are unusual in texture, visually interesting and a great talking point for your guests. Feel free to swap out any cheese you don't like for your own favourites, remembering that simplicity is key on this board.

Stack the crackers neatly around the cheeses, then place the grapes, physalis and candied pecans decoratively on the board. Serve alongside a small dish of honey or honeycomb.

pair with... This board would pair well with a quality sauvignon blanc, chablis or pinot grigio.

The Greek Meze board

Many holidays have been spent with my friends on the beautiful islands of Greece. The sensory overload of the aromas, colours, tastes and textures of Greek food takes me back to those happy times. Play some Greek music in the background and say yamas! with a few shots of ouzo.

ingredients

200g tzatziki (see recipe on page 160)

200g hummus (see recipe on page 150)

185g mixed Greek olives (I used Kalamata and garlic stuffed)

100g jarred quartered artichokes

85g caper berries

6 wholemeal pitta breads

200g Mediterranean falafels

100g mixed mini peppers

250g red grapes

150g green grapes

2 whole figs

60g radishes

135g cherry tomatoes

½ a lemon, to garnish

Greek Salad (see recipe on page 154)

For the souvlaki

500g pork

1 red onion

2 bell peppers

1 tbsp olive oil

2 tbsp dried oregano

method

To make the souvlaki, cut the pork into cubes. Peel the onion, deseed the peppers and cut them into similar-size pieces. Slide the pork, onion and peppers onto skewers, alternating between the three, then brush with olive oil. Heat a medium frying pan and cook the skewers for about 15 to 20 minutes until golden brown and cooked through. Sprinkle the souvlaki with the oregano and season to taste.

You will need a round tray or board approximately 35cm in diameter to build your meze platter. First, decant the tzatziki and hummus into ramekins and place them on your board.

Put the olives, artichokes and caper berries into more ramekins or small bowls and add these to your board. Meanwhile, warm the pittas in the oven for 5 minutes or briefly toast them.

Arrange the souvlaki on your board and place the warm pittas next to the souvlaki. Add the falafels and mini peppers to your board in neat stacks.

Wash the grapes and arrange them in a gap on your board. Halve or quarter the figs, slice the radishes, leave the cherry tomatoes whole and place them all on your board.

Slice the lemon into wedges and tuck them into a gap, for squeezing over the souvlaki. Add the Greek salad to your board, or serve it on the side in a separate bowl. Fill a pitta with your favourite meze combo and enjoy!

pair with...

Ouzo, Metaxa, Mythos beer or a 'Sexy Greek' cocktail (freshly squeezed orange juice and ouzo) are all great drinks to enjoy here, and no Greek feast would be complete without baklava for dessert.

The Hail Caesar board

This colossal Caesar salad is perfect for summer evenings in the garden or a posh picnic on the beach. Simple yet so tasty! Add your favourite nuts or vegetables for a more individual take.

ingredients

2 slices of good white bread

4 tbsp olive oil

Sea salt and black pepper

4 chicken breasts

Pinch of Italian seasoning

4 eggs

100g bacon rashers

2 romaine heart lettuces

1 avocado

20g parmesan

Cheese straws (see recipe on page 170)

175ml Caesar dressing

method

First, make the croutons by cutting the bread into small cubes. Place them in a bowl, drizzle with a little olive oil and season with salt and pepper. Tip the croutons into a frying pan on a medium heat and stir as they toast until golden brown on all sides. Transfer them onto a piece of baking paper in a single layer to cool and crisp up. These will keep for about 2 weeks in a Kilner jar or similar.

Brush the chicken breasts with some olive oil, then sprinkle with the Italian seasoning. Cook them in a preheated oven at 180°c until golden and cooked through. Leave to cool, then thinly slice the chicken breasts.

Hard boil the eggs until done to your liking, then leave to cool before peeling and slicing. Fry or grill the bacon until crispy.

Thoroughly wash the lettuce, pat dry and then arrange in a fan on the bottom of a circular board approximately 40cm in diameter. Arrange the sliced chicken breast and bacon above the lettuce.

Halve the avocado, remove the stone and place one half in the centre of the board as it is. Cut the other half into thin slices, removing the skin, and arrange on the edge of the board.

Place the sliced boiled eggs in a neat stack on your board. Use a cheese knife to shave the parmesan into a neat pile on the board. Arrange the cheese straws next to the sliced avocado. Scatter the croutons into any gaps, then serve your board with the Caesar dressing on the side.

pair with... Try a crisp white wine such as a pinot grigio or Spanish albariño. Belgian blonde lager would be a great alternative if beer is your preference.

The Burst of Energy board

Perfect on its own or as an accompaniment to the other boards in this book, this vibrant and healthy platter is full of vitamins which can lift the mood and provide energy. It can be enjoyed any time of the year but is at its best during summer when it makes a refreshing change from a simple salad.

ingredients

1 head of chicory, separated into leaves

100g purple sprouting broccoli

115g rainbow carrots

65g asparagus

30g celery with leaves

200g fine green beans

50g red cabbage, sliced

50g baby peppers

50g baby sweetcorn

75g baby cucumbers

25g radishes

50g cherry tomatoes

50g edamame beans

Fresh viola flowers and cress, to garnish

method

You'll need a round board approximately 30cm in diameter for the best results. Working your way around the edge, place the chicory leaves at equal intervals of approximately 3cm on the board. Lay them with the stems in the centre and the leaves pointing outwards to form the 'burst' effect.

Repeat this process with the broccoli, carrots and asparagus. Arrange the celery in the same way, choosing smaller sticks with the leaves still attached and showing as much greenery as possible.

Fill the remaining gaps around the board with the green beans and red cabbage. Slice the baby peppers into quarters, deseed them, then arrange in the center of the board at intervals of approximately 2cm. Do the same with the baby sweetcorn and baby cucumbers, without deseeding.

Halve or slice the radishes and cherry tomatoes then dot these around the board, working from the centre outwards. Scatter the edamame beans over the top, again from the centre outwards.

Garnish your board with the viola flowers and cress, then it's ready to serve. You could accompany this with one of the hummus recipes in the book (see pages 148 and 150) or buy your favourite hummus for dipping into.

pair with… If you're trying to remain health-conscious, a cucumber-infused water or spring water would be a refreshing drink for summer days alongside this board.

The Ibiza de dos Maneras board

This Spanish tapas board takes me back to Ibiza. The island is renowned for its huge club scene, but it also has a quaint old town with cobbled streets where you can spend the day slowly eating, drinking and watching the world go by.

ingredients

60g black Spanish olives

75g green Spanish olives

300g black sable grapes

150g cinnamon candied pecans (see recipe on page 176)

135g fresh figs

120g sun-dried tomatoes

75g membrillo (quince paste)

60g Ibérico cheese

60g Manchego

60g Spanish goat's cheese

150g Spanish omelette

80g serrano ham

75g Catalan fuet (dry-cured pork sausage)

65g chorizo d'Olot fort

50g paleta de cebo (Ibérico ham)

Sprigs of fresh oregano, to garnish

Rustic loaf of bread, to serve

Spanish olive oil and balsamic vinegar, to serve

method

You can make this board in two ways (de dos maneras); they use exactly the same ingredients but arranging them in different ways can transform the presentation.

To make a tapas style arrangement, set out three medium-size boards and a two-tiered tray. Decant the olives into two small ramekins or bowls, then place them on the top tray along with the grapes. Put the candied pecans, figs, sun-dried tomatoes and quince paste into more ramekins or bowls and place these on the bottom tray.

Slice the cheeses and Spanish omelette into triangular wedges, and arrange them together on one of the boards. On a separate paddle board, arrange all the cooked meats - sliced or rolled into cylinders - then garnish with the oregano. I have used a marble board here to show off the lovely colours of the charcuterie. Place the bread, oil and vinegar on the final board and serve.

To make a grazing board, put the olives, nuts, sun-dried tomatoes and quince paste into small bowls or ramekins and arrange them down the centre of a board approximately 50cm by 20cm.

Slice the Spanish omelette into wedges and arrange at the bottom of the board next to the bowls of quince paste and olives. At either end of the board, pile half the grapes in a neat stack. Alternate the cheeses and charcuterie across the board, tucking them in around the bowls or ramekins.

Garnish the board with the figs and oregano, then serve with bread, oil and vinegar on the side.

pair with...

Enjoy this feast with a glass of rioja, sangria, cava or a Spanish lager such as San Miguel. For a non-alcoholic option, Fanta Lemon is always a favourite in Spain.

The Signature Cheshire board

This is one of my favourite boards to make; it's my signature style, full of cheese produced in Cheshire, and all my favourite accompaniments are on there. The combinations work so well together: Orsom brie, local honey and walnuts is my perfect bite!

ingredients

65g walnuts

150g Nocellara olives

150g Orsom Breeze (British brie)

100g Orsom Woodew (smoked cheddar)

150g Hayfields Dairy Mature Cheddar Cheese

200g Cheshire Cheese Company Cheshire Truckle

75g Milano salami

1 yellow plum or fresh apricot

2 fresh figs

150g strawberries

200g red seedless grapes

80g raspberries

70g yellow cherry tomatoes

60g Miller's Plum & Date Toast

50g dried apricots

50g pistachios

50g redcurrants

30g blueberries

Local honeycomb, to serve

Mrs Darlington's Cheshire Chutney or homemade caramelised onion chutney (see recipe on page 162)

method

You will need a board or tray that is 35cm in diameter. I have used a tray as the deep sides hold everything in place. Put the walnuts and olives into small bowls or ramekins and place them on your board. Slice the brie into small sections and arrange around the olives.

Slice the cheddar cheeses into triangles and arrange them into a 'zip' pattern by alternating the triangles in opposite directions. Cut the Cheshire cheese truckle into small wedges and neatly stack them on your board.

Fold a slice of the salami in half and then half again. Repeat this with another slice, slot the two folded slices together and place them against the edge of the board. Do this with all the salami, arranging the pieces in a row. Place the plum or apricot centrally on your board.

Halve the figs, quarter the strawberries and place them both on your board. Cut the grapes into bunches of three or four and neatly stack them around the cheeses along with the raspberries.

Leave some of the tomatoes whole, slice some in half and arrange them all on your board. Stack the crackers in the remaining space and place the dried apricots in a row along the edge. Use the pistachios, redcurrants and blueberries to fill the gaps on your board.

Garnish the finished board with rosemary, oregano or any other foliage you have available. Serve with the local honeycomb and chutney of your choice.

pair with... As this is my signature board, I like to pair it with my most-loved drinks. Raspberry gin is a firm favourite, as is Prosecco. If I'm feeling fancy I may even have a glass of champagne!

The Sprezzatura board

This show-stopping Italian feast is perfect for entertaining friends and family, grazing away in the summer sunshine and relaxing with a drink or two. The board contains all my favourite Italian antipasto. Be a little sprezzatura and wow your guests with some Italian lingo too!

ingredients

280g parmesan

200g Nocellara olives

200g sun-dried tomatoes

1 tbsp balsamic vinegar

2 tsp green pesto

1 quantity of simple salad dressing (see recipe on page 156)

120g Milano salami

75g Gorgonzola

260g pearl mozzarella

15 basil leaves

60g breadsticks

1 head of chicory

1 fig

1 nectarine

2 apricots

30g rocket

80g coppa (dry-cured pork)

350g selection of tomatoes

200g red grapes

1 packet of crostini

6 asparagus spears

Fresh thyme and oregano, to garnish

method

First, grate 80g of the parmesan and scoop it onto a non-stick baking sheet in mounds of 2 or 3 tablespoons. Season with salt and pepper, then bake the grated parmesan in a moderately hot oven for approximately 18 to 20 minutes until melted and golden brown. Allow the parmesan crisps to cool on the tray before removing them carefully with a palette knife.

Place the cooled parmesan crisps in a stack on a board that is approximately 50cm by 30cm. Put the olives, sun-dried tomatoes, balsamic vinegar and pesto into more small bowls or ramekins and add these to your board. Decant the salad dressing into a small bowl or ramekin, slice the salami and arrange it around the salad dressing on the board.

Place the remaining parmesan, leaving the wedge intact, on your board along with the Gorgonzola.

Slide the pearl mozzarella onto small wooden skewers with a basil leaf between each ball. You should have enough to make three skewers.

Arrange the breadsticks in a neat stack on your board. Separate the chicory into individual leaves and place them next to the breadsticks. Halve the fig and place the pieces cut side up on your board. Slice the nectarine, remove the stone and arrange the pieces around the olives. Add the whole apricots.

Pile the rocket neatly in the corner of your board. Arrange the coppa (or any other cured meat of your choice) in an overlapping line on the diagonal. Slice the tomatoes and arrange on your board.

Add the grapes to your board and lay the crostini between the Gorgonzola and salami. Blanch the asparagus by dropping the spears into a pan of boiling water to cook for a few minutes, then transferring them straight into a bowl of iced water. Dry the spears then add them to your board. Alternatively, serve the asparagus raw.

Garnish your board with the fresh thyme and oregano, then it's ready to serve.

pair with...

This board would be great with an Italian lager like Peroni, a crisp Prosecco, or a bellini (the choice of cocktail or mocktail is up to you).

The Summer Cream Tea board

This cream tea with a twist is a quick and easy way to whip up a lunch for friends. Using a three-tiered serving tray adds that little touch of refinement to your grazing. Serve with scones and jam butters (see recipe on page 172) for the perfect summer afternoon treat.

ingredients

For the fruit tartlets

6 all-butter tartlet cases

60g fruit dip (see recipe on page 54)

20g mixed berries, thinly sliced

Mint leaves, to garnish

For the fresh fruit tier

20g physalis

20g blueberries

30g strawberries

60g each of raspberries and blackberries

150g red and green grapes

For the cracker tier

30g smoked salmon

30g cream cheese

30g Black Bob Extra Mature Cheddar

The Cherry Tree Cheeseboard Chutney

30g ham hock

The Cherry Tree Chilli & Pineapple Chutney

60g Orsom Breeze (British brie)

20g walnuts

Drizzle of honey

Fresh dill, cress and basil

8 Peter's Yard Original or Rye & Charcoal Sourdough Crackers

method

You'll need a three-tiered tray or cake stand to display this cream tea at its best. Start by filling the tartlet cases neatly with the fruit dip, then garnish with the sliced berries and mint leaves. Place these on the top tier of your tray. Next, arrange all the fresh fruit on the second tier of your tray.

Now make up your savoury cracker canapés. These are my favourite combinations: smoked salmon and cream cheese garnished with dill; cheddar and Cheeseboard Chutney garnished with cress; ham hock and Chilli & Pineapple Chutney garnished with basil; brie and walnut drizzled with honey.

Place the prepared crackers on the bottom tier of your tray, and serve the cream tea with freshly baked scones, clotted cream and jam or jam butters (see recipe on page 172).

pair with... A refreshing glass of Pimm's or champagne would make your cream tea complete. Alternatively, Twinings fruit or herbal tea is a lovely non-alcoholic option.

The Summer Breakfast board

This colourful spread contains all my favourite things to eat for an indulgent breakfast. You can pick and choose your preferred fruits and mix it up a little by adding some extras such as dried cranberries or nuts if you like. The combinations are endless!

ingredients

500g Greek yoghurt

280g quality granola (such as Dorset Cereals Honey Granola)

250g fresh cherries

200g blueberries, blackberries or both

200g melon

2 blood oranges

½ a conference pear

15g chia seeds

175g strawberries

50g fresh coconut

30g quality honeycomb

2 ripe bananas

method

Decant the yoghurt into a serving bowl and place on a rectangular board that measures about 50cm by 20cm. Put the granola, cherries (pitted first, if preferred) and blueberries or blackberries into more bowls. Arrange them along the board with space between each one.

Using a melon baller, scoop out spheres of the melon and put these in another small bowl to go on your board. Thinly slice the blood oranges and arrange them in a gap on the board itself.

Slice the pear from top to bottom and arrange in a fan on your board. Put the chia seeds into a small ramekin for sprinkling over the yoghurt and toppings.

Quarter the strawberries and arrange them on the board where there's space between the bowls. Peel the coconut into thin slices and layer these around the chia seed ramekin.

Put the honeycomb into a small dish with a honey drizzler or teaspoon. Finally, peel and slice the bananas then pile them neatly on your board in the remaining gap between bowls.

Serve your board with the honeycomb alongside and your breakfast is now ready for you to enjoy!

pair with... Freshly brewed coffee, your favourite cup of tea or a freshly squeezed orange juice are all winners to start your day right with this brilliant breakfast spread.

The Strawberry Fields board

A love of music, one of my favourite cities and a dear friend all inspired this board. It's full of British cheeses and locally grown strawberries from a nearby farm, and was one of the first themed boards I ever made.

ingredients

120g cream cheese (such as Philadelphia)

175g Parlick sheep's cheese

200g Beacon Fell Traditional Lancashire Cheese

1 Procter's Kick Ass Extra Mature Strong Cheddar

150g beetroot crackers

6 lychees

100g cherries

150g blackberries

150g raspberries

125g redcurrants

1 red apple

450g strawberries

method

Decant the cream cheese into a small ramekin or bowl and place on a board approximately 35cm in diameter. Slice the Parlick and Beacon Fell cheeses into triangles and arrange on your board in alternating directions. Slice the Proctor's cheddar truckle in half and place on your board.

Neatly stack the crackers on either side of the sliced cheese. Fill the gap between the cheeses with the lychees and cherries, arranging them in neat rows and working from the outside in.

On the opposite side of the board, make a neat row of blackberries. Stack the raspberries and redcurrants in the gaps around the edge of the board. Slice the apple then stack it back together and place on the board.

Fill the remaining central space on the board with strawberries, halved or quartered if preferred. Garnish the cream cheese with redcurrants and serve the board with your favourite chutney or pickles.

pair with... Take your pick from Liverpool gin, strawberry daiquiri, pink champagne or sparkling wine to accompany this deliciously fruity board.

The Tropical Fruit board

Summer holidays: long white sandy beaches and turquoise waters, the sound of the ocean and palm trees in the breeze. Sunshine by day and warm relaxing evenings. In summer, my favourite thing to eat is fresh fruit. This board is perfect for sharing with friends and family for an exotic island escape.

ingredients

1 whole pineapple

1 whole galia melon

150g blood orange

275g dragon fruit

200g watermelon

150g guava

100g papaya

100g kumquats

1 passionfruit

2 kiwis

2 yellow plums

8 lychees

65g physalis

45g strawberries

½ a pomegranate

method

You will need a tray that is approximately 40cm by 30cm, ideally with sides to hold all the fruit in. Start by cutting the pineapple in half down the centre. Scoop out the flesh from the two halves and cut into cubes. Put half of the cubed pineapple back into one of the outer shells and place this in one corner of your tray. Pile up a quarter of the remaining pineapple cubes in the opposite corner.

Halve the galia melon and use a melon baller to take out spheres of the fruit. Neatly stack half of the melon balls in a corner of your tray, and reserve the rest. Thinly slice the blood orange and arrange in an overlapping line on your tray. Cut the dragon fruit into quarters and arrange along one side.

Cut the watermelon into bite-size cubes, slice the guava, papaya and kumquats, then arrange them all on the tray along with the remaining melon balls. Cut the passionfruit in two and place the halves cut side upwards on the tray. Prepare the kiwis however you prefer and add them to the tray.

Place the yellow plums and lychees on your tray, leaving them whole. Fill all the remaining gaps with the physalis, strawberries, pomegranate seeds and the last quarter of cubed pineapple. Garnish the tray with any florals you have to hand, and your tropical fruit feast is ready to enjoy.

pair with...

Enjoy this board with a cocktail like a piña colada, mojito or margarita. Flavoured water or pineapple juice are great healthy alternatives.

The Summer Garland

This summer salad, arranged in a garland full of beautiful bright colours, is easy to prepare in just a few minutes. Add a splash of your favourite dressing and you're ready to go: a balsamic glaze would work well with this dish.

ingredients

25g pea shoots

160g red seedless grapes

200g strawberries

135g raspberries

70g feta cheese

25g mint leaves

Viola flowers, to garnish

Simple salad dressing (see recipe on page 156)

method

You will need a paddle board approximately 30cm in diameter. Start by placing the pea shoots in a ring around the board, leaving the centre circle clear.

Halve the grapes lengthways and arrange them on top of the pea shoots. Halve or quarter the strawberries, depending on their size, and distribute them around your garland.

Arrange the raspberries in the remaining gaps on your board. Cut the feta into small cubes and evenly dot them around the garland. Garnish with the mint leaves and viola flowers.

Serve the garland with a simple salad dressing of your choice, or a balsamic glaze.

pair with...

This simple salad is refreshing and light. A rosé wine, a crisp white and even a simple fruity or minty cocktail would pair well with this board.

The Summer Salad

This salad is perfect for grazing on with any of the summer boards in this book. You could also prepare your own salad dressing and add meat or fish to elevate it further for a light meal.

ingredients

2 little gem lettuces

2 heads of red chicory

4 baby cucumbers

6 spring onions

150g cherry tomatoes

200g green beans

50g red cabbage

175g edamame beans

Handful of cress, to garnish

method

Slice the lettuce and chicory, then mix them together in a large serving bowl. Slice the cucumbers, spring onions, tomatoes and green beans into bite-size pieces, then add them to your bowl.

Finely slice the red cabbage and toss everything together in the bowl to combine the salad. Scatter over the edamame beans and cress to finish.

My favourite combination of extras with this salad is tuna with mayonnaise, candied pecans and a balsamic glaze. I like to call it the New Yorker. Try creating your own combinations and see which one becomes your signature salad!

pair with...

Enjoy this summer salad with a crisp white wine, pale lager or any chilled soft drink of your choice.

Autumn

THERE IS NOTHING MORE REWARDING THAN PRESENTING A
PLATE OF FOOD THAT YOU HAVE PREPARED FOR YOUR FAVOURITE
PEOPLE TO SHARE, AND SEEING THE LOOKS OF JOY ON THEIR
FACES AS THEY ADMIRE YOUR CREATION.

The Autumn Sunshine board

I love nothing more walks with my family, especially in autumn, hearing leaves crunch underfoot and seeing rays of sunlight shine through the trees on a bright but crisp day. This is a perfect post-walk snack to share with the family; the mild cheeses make it great for children too.

ingredients

100g Gruyère cheese

100g Beacon Fell Traditional Lancashire cheese

60g unshelled pistachios

50g almonds

100g Milano salami

Toasts or crackers (such as Miller's Plum & Date Toasts)

1 persimmon (also called sharon fruit)

1 whole red apple

1 whole nectarine

1 fresh apricot

8 dried apricots

10 blackberries

200g red grapes

150g black grapes

130g green grapes

3 physalis

1 jar of tomato & chilli chutney (see recipe on page 166)

method

Take a board or tray which is approximately 25cm by 35cm; I have used a tray here.

Slice the Gruyère into rectangles, and then cut each rectangle diagonally to make right-angled triangles. Arrange the Gruyère on your board or tray.

Slice the Lancashire cheese into triangles, leaving the bright yellow wax on for interest. Layer them on your board or tray to create a sunshine effect, or make your own design.

Place two or three ramekins on your board and fill them with the pistachios and almonds, or any nuts of your choice. To make this more child friendly, you could always add some chocolates such as Reese's Pieces and fill more ramekins with raw carrot batons and hummus.

Thinly slice the salami and arrange on your board.

Arrange the toasts or crackers into a neat stack and place them next to the cheeses.

Slice the persimmon into three rounds. Leave the apple, nectarine and apricot whole, or slice if preferred, and arrange all the fruit on your board.

Arrange the dried apricots and blackberries in neat stacks where they will provide a good colour contrast. Add the grapes and physalis to your board.

Decant the chutney into a small Mason jar or ramekin to serve on the side. Your board is now ready to enjoy.

pair with...

A cool cloudy apple juice or an Irish coffee would pair beautifully with this board, as would an oaky chardonnay.

The Pumpkin Spice board

Dark crisp nights, pumpkin spiced everything, apple bobbing and rustic autumn vibes make this board the perfect accompaniment to spooky celebrations. Share a savoury cheeseboard with friends while the children dress up and tuck in to all the sweeties.

ingredients

200g Mexican or spicy cheddar cheese

100g Red Leicester cheese

1 Petit Grey soft cheese (or another soft cheese of your choice)

1 tbsp raw honeycomb or 30g honey

1 clementine

215g black grapes

125g red grapes

50g dried or 2 fresh apricots

10 blackberries

3 physalis

2 fresh figs

40g pumpkin spiced nuts (see recipe on page 174 to make your own, or use any other nuts of your choice)

1 jar of green tomato or tomato & chilli chutney (see recipe on page 166)

1 seeded sourdough bloomer loaf, to serve

method

Take a board approximately 25cm in diameter.

Cut the cheddar into cubes and slice the Red Leicester into triangles, then arrange the cheeses in stacks on your board.

Leave the soft cheese whole and place on your board with the raw honeycomb on top, if using, or put the honey in a small pot with a drizzler on your board.

Slice the clementine in half, place it onto the board, then add the grapes, apricots, blackberries, physalis and figs in small stacks around the other elements.

Add the nuts to a ramekin or small bowl and decant the chutney into a small jar or ramekin. Your board is now ready to serve alongside the seeded sourdough bloomer.

pair with...

Enjoy this board with a dry cider straight out of the refrigerator, a zinfandel or a sparkling shiraz. Alternatively, a warming bowl of spicy pumpkin or butternut squash soup makes this a heartier meal.

The Swiss Alpine board

This was inspired by images of Fribourgeoise cows on the pastures of the green foothills in the Swiss Alps. Following production in local dairies, the large Swiss cheese wheels emerge with different flavours based on when the milk was produced; autumn milk, for example, produces a nuttier cheese.

ingredients

70g Gruyère cheese

70g Emmentaler cheese

80g good quality honey (I used pine honey)

50g Tomme Vaudoise cheese (or another small soft cheese of your choice, such as Brie)

30g hazelnuts (or any nuts of your choice)

30g cornichons, sliced

6 blackberries

135g red seedless grapes

40g raspberries

2 whole apricots

100g redcurrants

60g blueberries

Pinecones, to garnish

Icing sugar, to garnish

1 packet of sourdough crackers (such as Peter's Yard)

100g Lindt dark chocolate (optional)

method

Take a board which is approximately 25cm in diameter. Slice the Gruyère into rectangles, and then cut each rectangle into long strips and arrange on your board.

Cut the Emmentaler into rectangles and arrange them in a neat stack on your board. Decant the honey into a small ramekin. Slice the Tomme Vaudoise and arrange around the honey.

Add the nuts to a ramekin or small dish of your choice, do the same with the cornichons and then place both on the board. Place the blackberries around the nut ramekin.

Cut the grapes into bunches of 2 to 4 and arrange them around the cheeses. Place the raspberries and apricots on your board. Arrange the redcurrants and blueberries into neat stacks to almost fill the remaining space.

Arrange a few pinecones around the board for decoration. Use a honey drizzler to add a little honey to your board and sieve a little icing sugar over the berries and pinecones.

Arrange the sourdough crackers in a small bowl next to your board. For an extra sweet treat, add shards of Lindt Swiss chocolate.

pair with... A crisp glass of riesling would pair perfectly with this alpine spread, as would merlot or even champagne. An IPA, pale ale or hoppy beer also works well.

The Ploughman's Lunch board

The great British grazing classic. A ploughman's lunch is quintessentially British and makes me think of pub lunches as summer turns to autumn, sitting outside with friends and enjoying a drink or two. The best versions consist of good quality meat, classic British cheeses and fresh seasonal fruit and vegetables. This serves one person, so double up to make two boards.

ingredients

75g Red Leicester

45g Cheshire cheese

45g Lancashire cheese

45g cheddar

70g silverskin pickled onions

45g walnuts

1 large scotch egg

2 mini Melton Mowbray pies

2 slices of good quality ham

1 tomato (or 1 whole apple if preferred)

100g red grapes

2 radishes

2 gherkins

1 jar of piccalilli

1 jar of Branston Pickle

25g celery, with the leaves on

¼ loaf of crusty bread

Butter, to serve

method

Find a paddle board that is approximately 35m long and 15cm wide. Slice the Red Leicester into triangles and arrange these in alternate directions on your board. Place the Cheshire, Lancashire and cheddar cheeses around the board in large wedges.

Measure the pickled onions and walnuts into separate ramekins and place these on your board. Halve the scotch egg and place the pieces cut side up on your board. Halve the mini pork pies and add them to one end. Halve the slices of ham, roll them up and place next to the pies.

Slice the tomato or apple horizontally and place next to the scotch egg. Arrange the grapes and radishes on your board, halving the radishes if they are large.

Quarter the gherkins lengthways and place the pieces on the edge of the board. Decant some piccalilli and pickle into ramekins or small Mason jars to serve alongside the ploughman's lunch.

Finally, garnish your board with the leafy celery and serve it with the crusty bread and butter.

pair with... A classic British ale or lager pairs well with this British staple, but my favourite accompaniment has to be a refreshing glass of cider.

The Harvest Festival board

I remember Harvest Festival celebrations as a child; my school would be adorned with images of wheat, breads and autumnal vegetables. The fruits on this board and their colours - oranges and deep maroons - along with the grains and seeds in the bread and crackers take me back to those early happy memories.

ingredients

3 persimmons

200g granulated sugar

2 tbsp cinnamon

Drizzle of olive oil

2 whole Baron Bigod Brie (200g each)

15g flaked almonds

15g dried cranberries

Good drizzle of quality honey

8 whole figs

65g candied pecans (see recipe on page 176)

100g gherkins

1 whole sourdough loaf

1 packet of cheese and pumpkin seed crispbreads

3 baby cucumbers

5 apricots

150g cherries

75g blackberries

250g red grapes

10 physalis

2 sprigs of rosemary, to garnish

1 jar of fig jam, to serve

method

Preheat the oven to a moderate temperature while you slice the persimmons and combine the granulated sugar with the ground cinnamon. Lay the persimmon slices on a baking tray, drizzle them with a little olive oil and then sprinkle them with the cinnamon sugar. Bake for approximately 30 minutes before removing from the oven and leaving to cool.

Working with one at a time so they are ready for your guests as required, peel back the rind on the brie and place in a small ovenproof dish. Scatter the flaked almonds and dried cranberries on top, finish with a drizzle of honey, then bake the brie in the oven for approximately 10 to 15 minutes until the cheese is soft to the touch. Place the brie in its dish on a board or tray that is approximately 40cm by 30cm.

The figs can be served as they are, or cooked if you prefer. Quarter or halve them for either option. To bake the figs, drizzle them with some honey and place them in the oven at a medium heat for 15 to 20 minutes, or until sticky and soft. Transfer the cooked figs to a ramekin and place on your board.

Put the candied pecans into another ramekin and place on your board. Slice the gherkins, make a little packet of brown paper to hold them and put this next to the baked brie.

Cut the bread into roughly 4cm wedges and arrange them around one side of the brie, with the crackers on the other side.

Slice the baby cucumbers into quarters and arrange them on your board. Place the apricots, cherries and blackberries around the edge of the board in neat piles.

Fill the remaining gaps with the grapes and physalis, then add sprigs of rosemary to garnish. Serve your board with the fig jam and baked persimmon slices on the side.

pair with... Add a good quality Prosecco, pinot grigio or pinot noir to your table for an indulgent treat.

The Capri board

The island of Capri is famous for its stunning landscapes, designer boutiques and beautiful restaurants. I often make this single-serving board with all the delights of Italian antipasto and imagine myself relaxing on the Bay of Naples. If you don't have all the ingredients, simply swap them for items already in your refrigerator.

ingredients

1 ball of mozzarella

4 basil leaves

50g Parma ham

40g Italian crostini or crackers

35g tarallini

65g red pepper

120g tomatoes

2 tbsp green pesto

Handful of pine nuts

2 tbsp balsamic vinegar

10g rocket

60g mozzarella pearls

60g red grapes

50g cherries

Fresh oregano, to garnish

method

Take a small board or plate approximately 20cm in diameter. Thinly slice the mozzarella, place a basil leaf between each slice and arrange on your board.

Roll the Parma ham into cylinders and arrange on your board. Place the crostini or crackers in a neat stack in the centre, and do the same with the tarallini in the corner of your board.

Thinly slice the red pepper, halve or quarter the tomatoes (depending on their size) and arrange them around the cheese, ham and breads.

Put the pesto into a small ramekin or bowl and top with the pine nuts. Decant the balsamic vinegar into another small ramekin or bowl.

Pile the rocket in the corner of your board, add a neat line of the mozzarella pearls next to it and then arrange the grapes and cherries around the greens. Garnish your board with the oregano.

When you're ready to serve, drizzle the pesto over the mozzarella and basil and dip the mozzarella pearls, tomatoes and crostini into the balsamic vinegar.

pair with... A good quality sparkling wine or soft drink such as San Pellegrino Limonata would pair well with this light lunch board. Alternatively, a simple sparkling water lets the flavours of the board come through.

The Girls' Night In board

For International Women's Day, women's rights, women in business, stay at home mums, mums who work, mums who are ill, daughters, aunties, friends, those who fought for our rights, those who suffer, those who are no longer with us. This board is for all the inspirational women I know, have known or who have inspired me.

ingredients

40g olives

30g pistachios

85g Port Wine Derby Cheese

40g Peter's Yard Original Sourdough Crackers

50g Petit Grey soft cheese

100g Wensleydale with cranberries

½ a kiwi

100g red seedless grapes

60g cherries

55g blackberries

40g blueberries

Edible flowers and sprigs of rosemary, to garnish

Sweet compote such as cherry or blackberry, to serve (optional)

method

Pop the olives and pistachios into ramekins and place them on a board approximately 35cm by 15cm. Slice the Port cheese and arrange on your board. Fan out the crackers on either corner of your board.

Cut the Petit Grey into wedges and arrange them around the ramekin of pistachios. Dice the Wensleydale into bite-size cubes and stack neatly on your board.

Slice the kiwi using a small sharp knife, making diagonal cuts in alternate directions to make a pretty pattern. Mix the grapes and berries and arrange on your board in colourful piles between the cheeses. Garnish the board with any florals and fresh herbs you have available.

pair with... The fruity flavours of this spread work best with a good quality red wine, such as a cabernet sauvignon or shiraz.

The Fort of India board

This was inspired by special dinners out at my local Indian restaurant with my friends, where we love to catch up, eat good food and have a laugh. The vibrant colours, spices and opulent presentation set the scene for a lavish Indian-themed grazing banquet to enjoy at home.

ingredients

400g boneless chicken breast or thigh

250g paneer

5 bell peppers

2 tbsp olive oil

2 tbsp curry powder

1 tbsp ground turmeric

4 mini naan breads

50g Bombay mix

Raita (see recipe on page 160)

Turmeric hummus (see recipe on page 150)

Pickled vegetables (see recipe on page 164)

200g lime pickle or mango chutney

300g rainbow carrots

150g rainbow chard

100g red cabbage, shredded

75g iceberg lettuce, shredded

75g cucumber

250g heritage tomatoes

40g mini poppadoms

method

Find a circular board or tray that is 35cm in diameter. Start by making the chicken and paneer kebabs. Cut the chicken, paneer and bell peppers into cubes of roughly the same size, then thread the pieces onto metal skewers. Keep the chicken and paneer separate, or mix everything together if you like. Combine the olive oil, curry powder and turmeric in a small bowl. Use a pastry brush to coat all the kebabs in the marinade, then place them in a preheated oven at 180°c for about 30 minutes or until the chicken is cooked through and golden brown at the edges.

While the kebabs are cooking, warm the naan breads in the oven for 5 to 10 minutes. Allow them to cool slightly before placing on your board or tray.

Decant the Bombay mix, raita, hummus, pickled vegetables and lime pickle or chutney into ramekins with a spoon in each, then arrange them on your board.

Cut the carrots into quarters, slice the rainbow chard into batons then neatly stack them together on your board. Add the shredded cabbage and lettuce, then slice the cucumber and tomatoes and use them to fill the remaining gaps.

Once the kebabs are cooked, allow them to cool slightly before placing on your board. Serve with the mini poppadoms and garnish with any herbs or flowers you have to hand. Enjoy!

pair with...

This board needs a crisp, refreshing drink alongside such as Tiger Beer, pinot grigio or riesling.

The Autumn Garland

The colours, textures, flavours and aroma of this board are reminiscent of autumn evenings around the fire pit with friends, chatting and eating and having fun. You can use any of your favourite cheeses, fruits and berries to make this board: use the autumn colour palette and you can't go wrong.

ingredients

200g Red Leicester

90g oak smoked jalapeño and red pepper cheddar

20g thyme and oregano sprigs, to garnish

100g grapes

40g cherry tomatoes

35g cornichons

150g blackberries

90g raspberries

35g fresh cherries

80g pomegranate seeds

20g blueberries

20g physalis

1 jar of tomato & chilli chutney (see recipe on page 166)

Crackers of your choice

method

Take a paddle board or a circular board approximately 30cm in diameter.

Cut the Red Leicester into roughly 2cm squares and arrange them around the board, leaving the centre open to create a ring. This will form the shape of your garland.

Cut the oak smoked cheddar into small triangles and arrange them in the ring alongside the other cheese. Arrange the sprigs of thyme and oregano around your board.

Slice the grapes and cherry tomatoes in half and arrange them on top of the herbs. Slice the cornichons lengthways and add them to the garland.

Distributing the colours evenly, place the blackberries, raspberries and cherries onto the board. Scatter the pomegranate seeds and blueberries into any remaining gaps.

Lastly, remove the leaves from the physalis and add the fruits to your board. Serve the autumn garland with pumpkin spiced almonds (see recipe on page 174), the tomato & chilli chutney and crackers of your choice.

pair with... A shiraz or malbec would pair well here, as would a local gin and tonic, lager or ale. If you would prefer a hot drink for chilly days, try a raspberry tea.

The Little Sweetheart board

This board was inspired by my little girl, who loves anything pink and having tea parties with her teddy bears and dollies. Creating a board with simple ingredients is fun and a great activity for children to get involved with too.

ingredients

80g Tatton trail mix (see recipe on page 178)

30g hummus (see recipe on page 150)

30g fruit dip (see recipe on page 54)

30g cheese straws (see recipe on page 170)

4 mini wraps

2 Dairylea cheese slices

2 slices of quality boiled ham

50g green grapes

40g strawberries

40g raspberries

15g blackberries

20g gem lettuce

25g celery

15g yellow pepper

1 whole baby cucumber

1 cherry tomato

2 viola flowers, to garnish

method

Take a board or plate that is 20cm in diameter. I have used a vintage plate for a tea party theme. Fill small ramekins with the trail mix, hummus and fruit dip. Cut the cheese straws into child-friendly bite-size pieces and pile them neatly on the board.

Using a heart shaped cutter, press six hearts from the mini wraps, cheese slices and ham. Make sandwiches by layering a slice of cheese and a slice of ham between two wraps, repeating until all the heart shapes are used up. Arrange the sandwiches in a fan on your board.

Thread the grapes onto cocktail sticks or bamboo skewers to add an element of fun, and add these to your board. Quarter the strawberries then place them around the ramekin with the raspberries opposite. Add the blackberries in a neat stack.

Separate the lettuce leaves and thinly slice the celery, pepper and cucumber. Arrange the salad by placing the sliced veg in a neat line. Top with the halved cherry tomato and viola flowers to serve.

pair with... Let the little ones choose their favourite fruity cordial such as blackcurrant or summer berry, or treat them to a strawberry milkshake!

The Oktoberfest board

Oktoberfest is the Bavarian gathering in Munich celebrated annually by more than six million people with drinking, eating and fun. This board takes me back to being with friends in the Hofbräuhaus, a famous tavern, clapping hands on the table, drinking steins of lager and eating the most amazing warm baked pretzels and bratwurst.

ingredients

20 chipolatas

4 large fresh pretzels

8 baby cucumbers, quartered (or gherkins if preferred)

2 white onions, thinly sliced

1 jar of pickled red cabbage (see recipe on page 164 to make your own)

For the beer cheese dip (obatzda)

200g spreadable cheese (such as Laughing Cow or Dairylea)

200g brie or Camembert

30g butter

4 tbsp German beer (I used Hofbräu)

2 tbsp Worcestershire sauce

2 tbsp Dijon mustard

1 tbsp paprika

½ tbsp chopped fresh chives

Salt and pepper, to taste

method

Preheat the oven to 180°c and lay the chipolatas on a baking tray. Cook in the centre of the oven for 25 to 30 minutes, turning halfway through. Allow to cool then transfer to a small serving dish.

Arrange the pretzels on a board or tray approximately 40cm by 30cm. Slice the cucumbers or gherkins into quarters and arrange them in a ramekin on your board or tray.

To make the beer cheese dip, simply combine all the ingredients until thoroughly mixed, reserving half of the chives for garnish. Serve in an interesting bowl or fondue pan, sprinkled with chives and a pinch of paprika. If you're making the ahead and storing the dip in the fridge, allow it to sit at room temperature for 30 minutes before serving.

Place the beer cheese dip on your board along with more ramekins or small bowls containing the white onion and pickled red cabbage, then you're ready to serve.

pair with... You can use any of your favourite beers in the dip and then enjoy the rest with the board! A German blonde ale is perfect for this recipe, but dark ales work equally well if you enjoy the bitter flavour. Alternatively, riesling would pair well with this board.

The Breakfast by the Bay board

This simple yet filling board is perfect for a relaxed Sunday brunch. Bagels are a breakfast staple in our house; the combination of chewy dough and toasted crispy crust is always a hit. We love to eat them with lots of different toppings and fillings like the ones here.

ingredients

55g bacon rashers

1 egg

1 avocado

1 red onion

1 beef tomato

4 baby cucumbers

4 radishes

A little of everything seasoning (see recipe on page 158)

Drizzle of honey

150g goat's cheese

4 bagels

100g Emmentaler cheese

50g fresh blackberries

120g German Brunswick ham

120g smoked salmon

20g rocket

10g cress

145g cream cheese

Fresh dill, to garnish

Sea salt

method

First, prepare your ingredients. Cook the bacon until crispy. Hard boil the egg, then leave to cool before peeling and slicing. Peel and thinly slice the avocado and red onion, using a mandoline for the onion if you have one to get really thin slices. Thinly slice the tomato, baby cucumbers and radishes.

Scatter some 'everything seasoning' onto a piece of baking paper, then drizzle some honey over the goat's cheese. Roll the goat's cheese in the seasoning so it sticks to the honey, then cut into slices.

Slice the bagels in half and place them on a board that is approximately 50cm by 20cm. Arrange the Emmentaler on a corner of the board. Stack the blackberries, sliced tomato and goat's cheese.

Roll the ham and smoked salmon into cylinders and place on the board. Arrange the boiled egg, avocado, rocket and cress around your bagels. Arrange the crispy bacon into a neat stack.

Place the radish, onion and cucumber in the top corner and garnish with fresh dill. Decant the cream cheese into a ramekin and sprinkle with sea salt. Add any additional toppings such as fruit or jams of your choice to the board before serving.

pair with... A cup of freshly brewed coffee, your favourite tea, or a cool glass of apple or orange juice all go very well with this breakfast spread.

The Autumn Salad

Nothing says autumn like butternut squash. This salad is perfect as a standalone dish or as an additional accompaniment to your autumn graze boards. Simple and easy to make, you can change any of the ingredients you don't like or leave out the bacon for a vegetarian option.

ingredients

800g butternut squash

200g cavolo nero

200g bacon lardons

120g spinach

50g croutons

20g dried cranberries

For the salad dressing

100g olive oil

3 tbsp apple cider vinegar

20g mustard

1 tbsp maple syrup

¼ tsp salt

Pinch of pepper

method

Cut the butternut squash into roughly 3cm chunks and place on a baking tray. Drizzle with a little olive oil and season to taste with salt and pepper. Roast the butternut in a moderately hot oven for around 30 minutes, or until golden brown and soft to the touch. When cooked, leave it to cool.

Meanwhile, bring a pan of water to the boil then drop in the cavolo nero and cook for about 5 minutes. Drain in a colander then rinse under cold running water to keep the leaves from overcooking. Drain again and set aside.

Place a frying pan on a medium-high heat and cook the bacon lardons for approximately 10 minutes until golden brown. Transfer them to a plate lined with paper towels to absorb the excess fat, and leave to cool.

To make the salad dressing, decant the olive oil into a jug. Stir in the vinegar, substituting the apple cider with red or white wine vinegar if you prefer. Add the mustard, maple syrup, salt and pepper to taste. Give the mixture a good stir and check you're happy with the balance of flavours.

Place the cooled butternut squash, cavolo nero, bacon lardons and spinach into a large serving bowl. Mix the ingredients together and top with the croutons and dried cranberries. You could also add chopped nuts here if you like. When you're ready to serve the salad, pour over the dressing and season to taste.

pair with...

Enjoy this salad with your favourite wine, beer or soft drink: it really does pair well with anything.

The Luck of the Irish board

I love spending time in Dublin with my husband and children. As it's just a short flight from Liverpool, we've had numerous day trips there over the years. I love the Irish bars and cobbled streets, and the National Leprechaun Museum was a family favourite!

ingredients

225g Cashel Blue (Irish blue cheese)

250g Coolea (Irish hard cheese)

250g Gubbeen (Irish semi-soft washed rind cheese)

1 whole pear

1 packet of Peter's Yard Original Sourdough Crackers

150g seedless green grapes

85g nuts of your choice

15g sage, to garnish

Caramelised onion chutney (see recipe on page 162)

Rustic bread, to serve

method

Place the Cashel Blue and Coolea cheeses, cut into quarters or large wedges, on a round board approximately 30cm in diameter.

Cut the rind off the Gubbeen in one piece, then cut the cheese into cubes. Place the rind on the board and pile the cubes of cheese back inside it.

Either leave the pear whole, or slice and arrange on your board. Neatly stack the crackers and grapes around the cheeses. Put the nuts into a ramekin or small bowl and garnish your board with the sage.

Serve your board with the bowl of nuts, caramelised onion chutney and sliced bread on the side.

pair with... It has to be a glass of Irish whiskey, a Guinness or a Baileys Irish Cream with this board!

Winter

THERE ARE NO RULES FOR CREATING A CHEESEBOARD OR GRAZING
PLATTER; IF YOU LOVE THE ELEMENTS THAT ARE ON THERE - THE
FLAVOURS, TEXTURES AND COMBINATIONS - THEN THAT'S ALL
THAT MATTERS.

The Festive Feast board

I love to shop for unusual or different cheeses at Christmas time. I gather my favourite people and we chat, drink and indulge, creating the perfect bite while playing card games and drinking champagne. I have specifically chosen British cheeses that I love for this board.

ingredients

155g Nocellara olives

100g redcurrants

60g hazelnuts

50g almonds

55g dried cranberries

1 Godminster Organic Vintage Cheddar Star

125g Parlick Fell sheep's cheese

180g Wensleydale cheese with cranberries

150g Kidderton Ash goat's cheese

1 Isle of Kintyre Christmas Pudding Cheese (a mature Scottish cheddar)

180g Milano salami

1 nectarine

1 clementine

1 red apple

3 whole apricots

550g green and red grapes

100g cherries

60g raspberries

2 whole figs

2 plums

50g dried apricots

90g good quality chocolate

method

A lazy Susan or a circular cheeseboard around 45cm in diameter is ideal for this feast. Place enough ramekins and bowls on the board to hold the olives, redcurrants, nuts and dried cranberries.

Cut the Godminster cheese into three sections, slicing horizontally so each one is star-shaped, and place them on your board. Slice the Parlick Fell and the Wensleydale into triangles and arrange them each in alternating directions. Cut the Kidderton Ash into little rounds and overlap them in a line around the edge of the board, then place the Isle of Kintyre cheese somewhere in the centre.

Take two slices of salami and fold them into each other so they meet. Repeat this four times, then pierce the salami folds through the centre with a cocktail stick or short wooden skewer to hold them all together. Do the same with the remaining salami and place the 'ruffles' on either side of your board.

Place the nectarine, clementine, apple and whole apricots around the edge of your board. Arrange the green and red grapes on opposite sides of the board to create nice colour contrasts.

Pile the cherries, raspberries and figs into the spaces on your board. Sit the plums next to the Kidderton Ash, then fill the remaining gaps on your board with dried apricots and the chocolate of your choice.

Serve the festive feast board with your favourite crackers, bread and chutney. I like to add a cranberry, cashew and raisin bloomer with some wholewheat crackers. Swap the suggested nuts for any of your favourites (see the recipes on page 174-176) and substitute any cheeses that you don't like or can't find.

pair with... This luxurious board goes well with a pink champagne such as a rosé Damien-Buffet, a glass of mulled wine, or a fun and fruity cocktail like a Woo Woo.

The Brie Bouquet board

This rustic board is full of warmth to cosy up with in winter. Ingredients can easily be swapped so all your favourites are on there, and it's a perfect sharing board for two. The bright colours, frosted berries and decorative florals make it look almost too good to eat.

ingredients

200g good quality brie

100g pumpernickel, sliced

45g Miller's Plum & Date Toasts

25g dried orange slices (see recipe on page 182)

1 whole pear, sliced

1 fresh fig, quartered

100g cherries

100g red seedless grapes

30g seedless green grapes

25g physalis

25g blueberries

65g blackberries

80g Nocellara olives

25g candied pecans (see recipe on page 176) or any nuts of your choice

60g frosty cranberries (see recipe on page 180)

60g dried apricots

35g raw honeycomb

15g sage leaves and florals, to garnish

method

You will need a board that is 30cm by 25cm. Place the brie in an ovenproof dish, ready to heat before serving. Leave a space for this dish in the bottom corner of your board.

In the top corner of your board, arrange the sliced bread into a fan shape and do the same with the toasts around the space for the brie ramekin. Add the oranges slices to either side of your board.

Spread all the fresh fruits, berries, olives, nuts, frosty cranberries and dried apricots across your board between the bread and crackers. Garnish with the sage and florals of your choice.

Lastly, place the brie in a preheated oven to cook at 180°c for 15 minutes, or until melted. Put the dish into the space on the board and top the melted brie with the honeycomb, plus florals to garnish.

pair with... This cosy sharing board is best with a good quality red wine like a merlot, or a white chardonnay.

The Bavaria board

Neuschwanstein Castle in Bavaria, which appears in the film Chitty Chitty Bang Bang, has been a place of enchantment since I was a young child. I would love to visit one day and enjoy the rugged hillsides and historical magnificence of this beautiful place.

ingredients

175g cambozola

160g montagnolo affine

150g Bavarian smoked cheese

145g cornichons

80g candied pecans (see recipe on page 176)

150g German salami

50g Peter's Yard Original Sourdough Crackers

1 whole apricot

150g red seedless grapes

130g cherries

75g blackberries

60g blueberries

50g physalis

Shards of dark chocolate (optional)

Edible flowers and sprigs of rosemary, to garnish

method

Slice the cambozola and montagnolo affine cheeses in half, cut the Bavarian cheese into small wedges, and arrange them all on a 25cm diameter board.

Put the cornichons and pecans into ramekins and place them on the board. Fold a slice of the salami in half and then half again. Repeat this with another slice, slot the two folded slices together and place them against the edge of the board. Do this with all the salami, arranging the pieces in a row.

Stack the crackers next to the salami and add the whole apricot to your board. Arrange the grapes, cherries and berries in neat stacks around your board.

Finish by filling the remaining spaces with the physalis, adding the dark chocolate, if using, and garnishing with the edible flowers and fresh rosemary.

pair with... A quality Bavarian beer such as Hofmeister, a white wine such as Müller-Thurgau or a quality riesling would pair well with this board.

The Edam & Gouda board

Edam and Gouda are some of my favourite cheeses, both originating from The Netherlands. The two towns that produce them are on my list of places that I would love to visit one day! Dutch stroopwafels are also a family favourite, enjoyed with a cup of coffee or tea.

ingredients

265g Gouda

160g Leerdammer

120g Edam

7 mini stroopwafels

4 squares of Lindt milk chocolate

4 Van Strien Meerzaden Stengel Multi Seed Straws, or homemade cheese straws (see recipe on page 170)

50g redcurrants

8 blackberries

50g raspberries

50g blueberries

1 tiger bread baton

1 red apple

30g hazelnuts

Rosemary or any other fresh herbs, to garnish

Butter and apricot jam, to serve

method

Take a board or tray that is approximately 50cm by 20cm. To prepare the Gouda, cut around the inside edge to remove the cheese from the rind and wax. Cut the Gouda into cubes and place the wax shell on the board with the cheese arranged inside.

At the opposite end of your board, fold each slice of Leerdammer in half and layer them up. Cut the Edam into triangles and arrange them on your board, overlapping in a diagonal line.

Place the stroopwafels next to the Edam, then break the chocolate into shards and arrange it next to the waffles. Place your multi seed or cheese straws near the Gouda in a corner of the board.

Divide the redcurrants into two equal piles and neatly place the bunches on either side of your board. Arrange the blackberries, raspberries and blueberries in neat piles or mix up the colours if you like, to add more interest.

Slice the tiger bread and place on your board. Slice the red apple horizontally and stack it in a corner. Finally, add the hazelnuts and garnish with the sprig of rosemary. Serve your board with the butter and apricot jam to eat with the bread and cheese.

pair with... This board is perfect for breakfast or lunch with the family as the cheeses are mild. A cup of your favourite coffee or tea would complement it beautifully, as would a glass of freshly squeezed orange juice.

The Chocolate Sweet Treat board

This dessert board is perfect for Christmas, New Year, or any celebration where sweet treats are a must. A chocolate lover's dream! The shortbread can be cut into different shapes for your occasion, and more fresh fruit or fruit dips can be added for a lighter board.

ingredients

260g chocolate hazelnut dip (see recipe on page 184) or melted chocolate

200g chocolate brownies

150g strawberries

5 shortbread stars (see recipe on page 168)

130g biscotti

1 apple, sliced

200g Spanish candied fruits

30g dark chocolate (or chocolate bark, see recipe on page 186)

75g salted pretzel sticks

85g dried apricots

30g walnuts

Icing sugar, to serve

method

Put the chocolate hazelnut dip and brownies into separate ramekins or small bowls, then place them onto a board or tray. Quarter the strawberries and arrange them next to the brownie ramekin.

Place the shortbread stars around the brownie ramekin and neatly stack the biscotti and apple slices in the remaining central space on the board. Fill in the gaps with the candied fruits and chocolate.

Arrange the pretzel sticks next to the dish of chocolate hazelnut dip, then add the dried apricots and walnuts to your board. Dust everything with icing sugar to finish.

For an extra indulgent treat, serve this board with the chocolate salami on page 188.

pair with... Take your pick of zinfandel, shiraz or sherry for a festive tipple to accompany this dessert feast.

The Fireside Fondue board

I love to make fondue for sharing with friends, especially during the winter months when we meet for a catch up and drink a few glasses of wine by the fire. Fondue is also a perfect way of using up Christmas leftovers from your cheeseboards, or any cheeses in your fridge with a short shelf life.

ingredients

For the accompaniments

85g tenderstem broccoli

100g purple broccoli

100g asparagus

100g cauliflower

2 tbsp olive oil

75g baby sweetcorn

100g cherry tomatoes

1 loaf of sourdough bread

For the fondue

150g Gruyère

150g Emmentaler

150g Gouda

2 tbsp cornflour

250ml vegetable or chicken stock

1 tbsp garlic powder

1 tsp Dijon mustard

Pinch of nutmeg

method

For the accompaniments

Blanch both types of broccoli, the asparagus and the cauliflower (broken into florets) in a pan of boiling water for a few minutes before draining and transferring straight into a bowl of iced water.

Heat the olive oil in a frying pan and gently fry the baby sweetcorn for about 5 to 8 minutes, until tender and golden. Arrange the prepared vegetables, including the cherry tomatoes, on a board or in a bowl of your choice. Slice the bread into bite-size pieces and place in a basket or bowl to serve.

For the fondue

Grate all the cheeses into a bowl and add the cornflour. Toss until all the cheese is properly coated. Pour the stock into a saucepan over a medium heat and add the cheese mixture a little at a time, stirring well so the cheese is thoroughly melted before adding the next batch.

Once all the cheese has been added and has melted, stir in the garlic, mustard and nutmeg to taste. Carefully pour the fondue into a fondue pot and use forks or skewers to dip your accompaniments in.

pair with... Try white wines such as rieslings, kirsch or herbal tea with this board.

The Tête de Moine board

I have been intrigued by Tête de Moine cheese since seeing it on a cookery programme many years ago. The delicate curls you can create with it, using a special device called a girolle, are a real talking point at any special occasion, and there's something very therapeutic about curling the cheese too!

ingredients

1 Tête de Moine (900g)

2 whole pears

100g physalis

100g red seedless grapes

1 packet of Miller's Toast

Frosty cranberries (see recipe on page 180)

Your favourite chutney, to serve

method

Set up the Tête de Moine with a girolle (a device which you attach to the cheese and turn to scrape curls of cheese from the surface) in the centre of a circular board.

Place all the accompaniments on the board, or decant them into separate ramekins or small bowls for serving alongside the cheese.

You can add any of your own favourite accompaniments to this board, as it really is about the cheese being the star of the show.

Serve with a loaf of rustic cranberry and walnut bread alongside your chosen chutney.

pair with... Depending on the time of year, although I do think this cheese is best suited to winter months, this board would be perfect with a great red wine such as a bordeaux or chablis. Alternatively, try a crisp white like a pinot grigio.

The Little Star board

This colourful star-themed board is perfect for little grazers. With all my daughter's favourite after school treats included, this board is great for snacking or for teatime with her friends.

ingredients

150g French baguette

75g cream cheese or hummus (see recipe on page 150)

20g red pepper

15g celery

25g carrot

25g cheddar

130g watermelon

115g cantaloupe melon

45g kiwi

½ an apple

50g blueberries

15g strawberries

75g quality ham

75g Tatton trail mix (see recipe on page 178)

method

First, hollow out the baguette and slice diagonally into 4 pieces. Fill the hollow centres with cream cheese or hummus. Slice the pepper, celery and carrot into thin batons and stick them into the filled baguettes so they resemble little sail boats. Place these on a round board about 30cm in diameter.

Cut the cheddar, both types of melon and the kiwi into slices and then press out star shapes using a small cutter or a sharp knife. Place the apple half face down in a dish (star-shaped would be ideal).

Using bamboo skewers with loops at the end so there are no sharp points, thread the fruit stars and berries onto the skewers in colourful patterns. Start with the watermelon and leave 2cm of space at the pointed end. Push this end of the skewers into the apple half to hold them in place.

Arrange the ham in the dish, then fill it with the remaining fruit and cheese. Serve with a ramekin or small bowl of your little one's favourite trail mix.

pair with... This board pairs well with a cold glass of milk, a milkshake or a glass of fruit cordial.

The Love of Scotland board

Scotland holds a very special place in my heart. It's where my husband and I got married, and where we spent many special holidays with friends. The breathtaking scenery, the history and amazing distilleries mean that you never have the same experience twice. This board pays homage to Scotland through some of its beautiful cheeses.

ingredients

20g walnuts

50g honeycomb or Scottish heather honey

100g Scottish oatcakes

1 whole pear

110g Caboc double cream cheese

200g Arran oak smoked cheddar

1 Connage Clava Brie (optional)

150g green grapes

Thistles or eryngium flowers, to decorate

method

Put the walnuts and the honeycomb or Scottish heather honey into small ramekins and place on a small board, about 30cm by 17cm. Arrange the Scottish oatcakes in a fan at the top of your board.

Thinly slice the pear and arrange on your board. Slice the Caboc and arrange around the ramekin of honey. Cut the Arran cheddar into small wedges and arrange on your board. If using the Clava Brie, slice the log into rounds and add to your board.

Arrange the grapes in neat stacks to fill the remaining gaps on your board, and then garnish with fresh herbs or decorate with florals. You could also add some blackcurrants or dried apricots to this rustic board for a great colour contrast and fruity burst of flavour.

pair with... Enjoy this board with a fine Scottish whisky, a smoky old fashioned or a Drambuie cocktail.

The Winter Celebration board

Christmas, New Year's Eve, birthdays, anniversaries… if you're celebrating any occasion, this indulgent board is perfect for gatherings of family and friends. The combination of savoury cheeses and sweet treats makes it a sure winner.

ingredients

150g quality olives

65g candied pecans (see recipe on page 176)

150g chocolate hazelnut dip (see recipe on page 184)

200g Cheshire Cheese Company Black Truffle Cheddar Cheese

200g truffle-infused brie

250g Camembert

200g Comté cheese

120g Manchego

100g bresaola

100g Milano salami

70g breadsticks

120g shortbread biscuits (see recipe on page 168)

30g dried orange slices (see recipe on page 182)

90g biscotti

100g physalis

120g raspberries, blueberries, blackberries or a mixture

200g cherries

250g strawberries

350g red and green seedless grapes

15g raw honeycomb

method

If you have one, a lazy Susan is ideal here, but if not you can use a normal circular board approximately 45cm in diameter. Start by decanting the olives, candied pecans and chocolate hazelnut dip into separate ramekins and placing them on your board.

Slice the black truffle cheddar into eighths and place on your board. Do the same with the truffled brie and the Camembert. Note that Camembert can be eaten at room temperature or heated just before serving. I prefer to bake it in an ovenproof dish for 15 minutes just before serving.

Slice the Comté cheese into batons, cut the Manchego into triangles and place them both on your board. Arrange the bresaola and salami around the olives and cheese. Stack the breadsticks and shortbreads at opposite ends. Arrange the orange slices and biscotti neatly on the board.

Fill all the remaining gaps with the fresh fruits and berries. Garnish your board with seasonal herbs or flowers of your choice, then serve with the honeycomb and your favourite chutney on the side.

pair with…

It's a celebration, so break out a bottle of champagne! I recommend Veuve Clicquot, Moët & Chandon or Bollinger. Cava or Asti sparkling wine are also great alternatives.

The Winter Garland

A festoon of festive favourites, this garland will be the centre of attention at any of your winter gatherings. It's an easy indoor activity to do with the family too; choose your favourite cheeses and accompaniments and create something magical together.

ingredients

40g rosemary sprigs

50g saucisson

2 fresh figs

3 slices of orange (fresh or dried)

30g Double Gloucester

65g cherries

50g raspberries

50g blackberries

50g mixed coloured grapes

90g olives

75g pearl mozzarella

125g redcurrants

1 packet of sourdough crackers (or any other crackers of your choice)

method

Take a paddle board or another circular board, approximately 30cm in diameter.

Evenly spread the rosemary sprigs around the edges of the board, leaving the centre open, to create a ring.

Slice the saucisson into small sections and evenly place them on top of the rosemary.

Cut the figs in half and space the pieces equally around the ring on your board.

Cut the orange slices into semicircles and arrange them around your board.

Use a small star cutter to cut the Double Gloucester into small stars. Alternatively, cut the cheese into small cubes around 2cm in diameter. Place the cheese stars onto your garland.

Arrange the cherries, raspberries and blackberries around your board, distributing the different colours evenly.

Halve the grapes vertically and add them to the garland along with the olives.

Scatter the pearl mozzarella around your board, filling in any remaining gaps in the ring.

Lastly, arrange the redcurrants around your board in small bunches.

Serve your winter garland with sourdough crackers and a sweet chutney of your choice.

pair with... A cabernet sauvignon, chardonnay or zinfandel would pair well with this dish, as would a mulled cherry punch.

The Winter Cheese Log board

Cheese logs are so simple to make, great as a standalone board but also for adding to any of your creations. This one uses cranberries and pecans and is ideal for festive gatherings. Just take a chunk, spread it on your favourite bread or crackers and you have comfort food at its best.

ingredients

150g dried cranberries

75g pecans, chopped

75g pistachios, chopped

4 tbsp chopped fresh chives

250g cream cheese (such as Philadelphia)

120g mature cheddar cheese, freshly grated

Drizzle of maple syrup (optional)

200g smoked bacon lardons (optional)

method

Set half of the cranberries, pecans, pistachios and chives to one side. Put the remaining half into a bowl with the cream cheese and grated cheddar, then mix thoroughly.

Lay out a long sheet of cling film on your worktop and decant the contents of the bowl into the centre. Shape the cheese mixture into a log of your preferred size by rolling it forwards, wrapping the log tightly in cling film as you go.

Keep the cheese log in the fridge until firm and ready for serving. Combine the ingredients you set aside earlier and scatter them evenly over a large plate or piece of baking paper. Roll the chilled log in the mix to cover the cheese and form an outer layer.

Serve on a seasonal board or plate and drizzle a little maple syrup over the top if you like for a further sweet kick. This would be perfect served with frosty cranberries (see recipe on page 180).

You can also add bacon lardons to the cheese log mix if you like, before shaping and chilling. Fry the lardons in a hot pan until golden, then tip them onto a plate lined with kitchen roll to absorb the excess fat. Leave the bacon to cool completely before adding to your cheese mixture. Other nuts also work really well here, such as walnuts or hazelnuts. For a deeper and tangier flavour, use a soft goat's cheese instead of the cream cheese.

pair with... Get even further into the festive spirit with a mulled wine, sparkling wine or champagne alongside this little treat.

The Yorkshire Lunch board

There are so many things I love about Yorkshire, one of my favourite places to visit in the UK, from York and Harrogate to the dales, forests, castles and abbeys. This board takes me back to lunches in beautiful country pubs, sitting by roaring fires and grazing the day away.

ingredients

100g lean beef mince

1 tbsp olive oil

2 mini slider buns

10g rocket

75g Wensleydale cheese

75g Shepherds Purse Yorkshire Blue cheese

50g Wensleydale cheese with cranberries

150g red and green seedless grapes

60g scotch eggs

25g walnuts

30g celery

40g piccalilli

40g pickled red cabbage (see recipe on page 164)

40g silverskin pickled onions

1 whole pear

100g artisan sausage rolls

Rakusen's of Yorkshire crackers

method

First, make the mini burgers. Shape the beef mince into two patties and heat the olive oil in a frying pan. Cook the patties over a medium to high heat for 15 to 20 minutes until golden on the outside and done to your liking. Place them in the slider buns (toasted if preferred) and top with rocket.

Take two boards of 35cm and 25cm in length, or one larger board that measures approximately 35cm by 30cm. Place the wedges of cheese on your board then arrange the grapes, scotch eggs and walnuts around them.

Slice the celery into batons and arrange on the board in a neat pile along with any remaining rocket. Put the piccalilli, red cabbage and pickled onions into separate ramekins and place on your board.

Fill the remaining gaps on your board with the pear, sausage rolls and crackers.

Serve the board with Wensleydale chutney for the cheeses and tomato ketchup for the burgers on the side, if you like.

pair with... This hearty lunch goes brilliantly with Yorkshire craft ale or a cup of freshly brewed real Yorkshire tea.

The Winter Salad

I adore Romanesco broccoli. The little florets look like Christmas trees, especially alongside pomegranate seeds which remind me of ruby jewels, and the crumbled feta that tops everything like snowflakes. Use this salad to accompany your winter graze creations or as a standalone dish for a light lunch or dinner. Add some roasted chicken for a more protein-rich meal.

ingredients

150g kale

250g Romanesco broccoli

200g pomegranate seeds

150g feta cheese, cubed

125g French dressing

Pinch of salt

method

Tear the kale into bite-size pieces and break the broccoli into florets. Blanch the kale and broccoli by bringing a large pan of water to the boil and dropping the greens into the pan to cook for 2 minutes. Remove with a slotted spoon and place straight into a bowl of iced water. Alternatively, both the kale and broccoli can be served raw.

Add the cooled and drained or raw kale and broccoli to a large serving bowl. Stir in the pomegranate seeds, then crumble the feta over the top, leaving a few cubes whole.

Decant the French dressing into a small jug so you can pour it over the salad according to taste. Add a little salt to the salad and toss everything together just before serving.

You could also add almonds or any other nuts for an extra crunch. To make this a more substantial meal without a graze board, brush two chicken breasts with melted butter or olive oil, season them with salt and pepper, then roast them in the oven at a moderate temperature for 20 to 30 minutes until golden brown. Leave the chicken to cool before slicing and adding to your salad.

pair with... Enjoy this salad with your favourite wine, beer or soft drink: this really is a dish that pairs well with anything.

The Pantry

ASK YOUR NEIGHBOURS WHETHER THEY GROW OR MAKE ANYTHING THAT COULD ENHANCE YOUR BOARDS IN EXCHANGE FOR SOME HOMEMADE GOODIES!

Simple Crackers

What happens on the days you really fancy some cheese and crackers, but you've run out or they have gone stale? Make your own, with the simplest recipe I have ever known!

Preparation time: 20 minutes | Makes 18

ingredients

3 slices of any bread

A little of everything seasoning (optional, see recipe on page 158)

method

Use any bread you have available; wholemeal and seeded loaves work particularly well. Cut the crusts off each slice. Using a rolling pin, roll the bread until thin and flat.

Cut the bread into pieces approximately 5cm square. To add extra flavour, you could drizzle a little olive oil and sprinkle some sea salt, dried herbs, chilli flakes or seasoning over the bread.

Place the squares on a baking tray lined with greaseproof paper and bake them in a preheated oven at 180°c for approximately 15 minutes.

Remove the crackers from the oven and leave to cool on a wire rack. Store in a Kilner jar for up to 1 week, if they last that long!

cook's tip... Seeded bread or pumpernickel would give your crackers interesting flavours. Try using a cookie cutter to shape them for something even more individual.

Green Tomato Bruschetta

This recipe uses heirloom tomatoes for something a little different than the red ones we usually see, but you can use ordinary vine tomatoes if green ones are out of season or unavailable. Don't mistake the heirloom variety for end of season green tomatoes, which taste more tart and bitter.

Preparation time: 15 minutes, plus 2 hours chilling | Makes about 10

ingredients

6-8 green heirloom tomatoes

2 tsp garlic powder

1 tbsp balsamic vinegar

2 tbsp olive oil

3 sprigs of fresh oregano (or 2 tbsp dried oregano)

8 basil leaves

½ tsp salt

Black pepper

1 baguette or ciabatta loaf

method

Slice the tomatoes, remove the centres and seeds, then cut the slices into 1cm cubes. Put the prepared tomato into a mixing bowl with the garlic powder, balsamic vinegar and half the olive oil. Finely chop the fresh oregano and basil, stir everything together, then add salt and pepper to taste.

Leave the bruschetta topping in the fridge for 2 hours so the tomatoes can absorb all the flavours, then remove 30 minutes before serving.

Slice the baguette or ciabatta and heat the remaining olive oil in a large frying pan. Lay the slices of bread into the pan and toast until crisp and golden.

Arrange the toasts on a board or platter and either place bowls of the tomato mixture on the side for people to make their own, or spoon it onto the bruschetta ready to serve. Garnish with a little more fresh oregano and basil if you like.

cook's tip.... You could add small cubes of mozzarella and a drizzle of balsamic glaze to this recipe for a bruschetta caprese.

Beetroot Hummus

This simple but colourful and tasty dip will elevate your crudités and any board that contains crunchy vegetables.

Preparation time: 1 hour 10 minutes | Makes about 375g

ingredients

4 beetroot

2 tins of chickpeas

2 cloves of garlic, peeled

6 tbsp tahini

6 tbsp olive oil

1 lemon, zested and juiced

½ tsp salt

method

Wash the beetroot and remove the stalks. Preheat the oven to about 180°c and bake the beetroot for about 1 hour, or until soft and cooked though. Leave to cool.

Drain and rinse the chickpeas, then set aside 3 tablespoons for garnish. Put the rest into a food processor along with the cooled beetroot, garlic, tahini, olive oil, lemon zest, juice, and salt.

Blend the mixture for a few minutes then check the taste and consistency, adding a little more oil or water if needed to loosen the hummus.

Serve immediately with the reserved chickpeas on top and a scattering of 'everything seasoning' (see recipe on page 158) or store the hummus in a Kilner jar. It will keep in the fridge for up to 3 days.

cook's tip.... You could try decorating the finished hummus with some fresh edible flowers as an alternative colourful garnish.

Golden Hummus

This easy but colourful and tasty side dish will elevate your crudités and any board that contains crunchy vegetables. To make a child-friendly hummus, simply omit the turmeric and nutmeg.

Preparation time: 1 hour 10 minutes | Makes about 375g

ingredients

2 tins of chickpeas

2 cloves of garlic, peeled

6 tbsp tahini

6 tbsp olive oil

1 lemon, zested and juiced

1 tbsp ground turmeric

½ tsp ground nutmeg

½ tsp salt

2 tbsps pickling spice, to garnish

method

Drain and rinse the chickpeas, then set aside 3 tablespoons for garnish. Put the rest into a food processor along with the garlic, tahini, olive oil, lemon zest, juice, turmeric, nutmeg and salt.

Blend the mixture for a few minutes then check the taste and consistency, adding a little more oil or water to loosen the hummus if needed.

Serve immediately with the reserved chickpeas on top and a scattering of pickling spice to garnish. Store the hummus in a Kilner jar. It will keep in the fridge for up to 3 days.

cook's tip... This is perfect served on flatbreads with avocado, feta and roasted tomatoes.

Simple Salad

This goes very well with the Smörgåsbord on page 40.

Preparation time: 5 minutes | Serves 4

ingredients

50g green apple

50g white cabbage

50g celery

50g green grapes

50g walnuts

15g fresh parsley

1 tbsp mayonnaise

1 tbsp Greek yoghurt

½ tbsp lemon juice

Salt and pepper, to taste

Handful of pomegranate seeds and dried cranberries (optional)

method

Core the apples, then thinly slice them into matchsticks and place in a large serving bowl.

Slice the white cabbage into thin shreds and add them to the apple.

Cut the celery into small slices, halve the grapes and add both ingredients to the bowl.

Crush the walnuts using the back of a spoon, finely chop the parsley and then fold them through the salad.

In a separate bowl, combine the mayonnaise, Greek yoghurt, lemon juice and seasoning. Pour this dressing over the salad and add more seasoning to taste.

Garnish with a handful of pomegranate seeds and dried cranberries for a beautiful finish.

cook's tip... Add some roasted chicken to elevate this take on a simple Waldorf salad even further.

Greek Salad

A lovely summery addition to any board, particularly The Greek Meze board on page 58.

Preparation time: 10 minutes | Makes about 300g

ingredients

½ a small red onion

½ a cucumber

100g feta cheese

50g cherry tomatoes

50g mixed Greek olives

2 tbsp olive oil

2 tbsp lemon juice

½ tbsp dried oregano

method

Thinly slice the red onion, then chop the cucumber and feta into cubes. Halve the cherry tomatoes and olives, or leave the latter whole if you prefer but remember to warn guests about the stones!

Place all the ingredients into a bowl and toss gently together. Taste to check the seasoning - you probably won't need salt because of the feta - and then serve, or cover and chill in the fridge until needed.

cook's tip... You could add shredded romaine lettuce to this salad for a cost-effective way to make it go further.

Simple Salad Dressing

Making a homemade dressing to add to your salads is simple, and healthier than shop-bought bottles. Experiment with flavours by combining red wine, white wine or apple cider vinegars with fresh herbs such as mint, dill and basil or finely chopped red chillies.

Preparation time: 5 minutes | Makes about 250ml

ingredients

5 tbsp olive oil

2 tbsp red wine vinegar

2 tbsp maple syrup

1 tbsp wholegrain mustard

Salt and pepper, to taste

method

Put all the ingredients into a jug and whisk to combine everything. Decant into a salad dressing bottle and store in the fridge. This will keep for 4 to 6 weeks.

Try swapping the maple syrup and mustard for 1 whole deseeded chilli and 2 sprigs of mint (finely chopped) along with the juice of half a lemon. Have fun and try your own combinations!

cook's tip... Making your own salad dressing can be more cost-effective and can also make a nice gift when decanted into a pretty bottle.

A Little of Everything Seasoning

This was inspired by 'everything bagel' seasoning. It's a simple mix that can be stirred into or sprinkled over cream cheese, bread dough, roasted vegetables, hummus, salads and much more, adding flavour and interest to your creations.

Preparation time: 2 minutes

ingredients

4 tsp white sesame seeds

2 tsp black sesame seeds

2 tsp poppy seeds

2 tsp garlic flakes

2 tsp onion flakes

1 tsp flaked sea salt

method

Measure the ingredients into a bowl and stir to mix them evenly. Use the seasoning on your creations, or make a larger batch and save for later in a Kilner jar or airtight container.

cook's tip... This seasoning works really well stirred into a savoury trail mix or added to fresh popcorn.

Raita & Tzatziki

These two yoghurt dips are very easy to make and so versatile, with just a few ingredients that differ to make great accompaniments to a variety of meals. It's just as nice simply served with warm pitta breads for an afternoon snack.

Preparation time: 10 minutes | Makes about 375g

ingredients

½ a cucumber

½ a green chilli

2cm root ginger, peeled

250g natural yoghurt (or Greek for tzatziki)

1 clove of garlic, crushed

½ a lime, juiced (or lemon for tzatziki)

50g fresh coriander, finely shredded

25g fresh mint, finely shredded

2 tbsp olive oil (for tzatziki)

½ tsp garam masala

½ tsp salt

method

To make raita, grate the cucumber into a bowl and then squeeze out the excess water using your hands or a clean tea towel. Grate the green chilli and root ginger into the bowl of drained cucumber. Stir in the yoghurt, crushed garlic and lime juice then add the shredded herbs, garam masala and salt. Decant the dip into Kilner jars to serve.

To make tzatziki, follow the instructions above but use the Greek yoghurt instead of natural and lemon juice instead of lime. Stir in the olive oil and leave out the garam masala. It should keep for the same amount of time in an airtight container in the fridge.

cook's tip...   This will keep for about 5 days in the fridge.

Caramelised Onion Chutney

I really enjoy tasting chutneys and pairing them with different cheeses. Every so often it's good to make my own, and this chutney also makes a perfect gift.

Preparation time: 1 hour 30 minutes | Makes 1 litre

ingredients

1.5kg onions

2-3 tbsp olive oil

300g dark muscovado sugar

200ml red wine vinegar

3 tbsp garlic powder

1 tbsp wholegrain mustard

½ tsp paprika

¼ tsp chopped fresh or crushed dried chillies

method

Thinly slice the onions with a mandoline so they are less than half a centimetre thick. Heat the oil in a large saucepan, add the onions and fry gently for around 30 minutes. The onions should turn almost translucent but not burn.

Stir in 3 tablespoons of the sugar, let the onions get some colour, then add the rest of the sugar after a few minutes. Stir all the remaining ingredients into the pan.

Simmer the mixture for 45 minutes until the volume of chutney has reduced by more than half. Make sure the chutney doesn't stick to the bottom of the pan by stirring occasionally.

Once cooked, spoon the chutney into sterilised Kilner jars, seal and store in a cool place. This chutney should keep for up to 6 months.

cook's tip... This chutney pairs particularly well with a mature cheddar cheese on a crisp sourdough cracker.

Pickled Vegetables

Pickling your own vegetables is easy, fun and a good way to use up produce that has a short shelf life. The vibrant colours add interest, flavour and an individual touch to your creations.

Preparation time: 30 minutes | Makes about 150g

ingredients

150g crunchy vegetables (such as red cabbage, carrots, baby cucumbers, cauliflower, turnip, beetroot, baby onions or even sprouts)

250ml water

1 tsp sugar (optional)

2 tbsp salt

2 tbsp pickling spice (usually contains coriander seeds, yellow mustard seeds, chilli flakes, ginger, bay, allspice, black peppercorns, and cinnamon)

250ml pickling vinegar

method

You will need a jar with a tight-fitting lid that holds at least 500ml. First, sterilise your jar by filling it with hot water then microwaving for a few minutes. Meanwhile, slice the vegetables of your choice and then pack them into the emptied sterilised jar. Leave enough space at the top for the pickling liquid to completely cover the vegetables.

Put the water, sugar and salt in a pan over a medium heat and stir until dissolved, then add the pickling spice and vinegar. Continue stirring gently and bring the liquid to a simmer, then remove the pan from the heat.

Pour the hot pickling liquid over the vegetables in the jars. Allow the contents to cool to room temperature before tightly securing the lids and placing the jars into the fridge. The pickled vegetables will keep like this for 2 to 3 weeks.

cook's tip... Have you tried pickling fruit? Grapes and cranberries pickle really well.

Summer Tomato & Chilli Chutney

In the summer I love to grow tomatoes and all sorts of berries and herbs. This recipe is perfect for using up all those ripe tomatoes so they can be enjoyed all year around.

Preparation time: 1 hour | Makes 1 litre

ingredients

500g ripe tomatoes

4 tbsp garlic powder

1 tsp ground ginger

300g soft dark brown sugar

150ml apple cider vinegar

4 tbsp crushed dried chillies

1 tsp coriander seeds

1 tsp mustard seeds

method

Add the tomatoes, garlic and ginger to a food processor and pulse until the tomatoes are finely chopped. Transfer the mixture to a saucepan and add the remaining ingredients.

Bring to the boil and allow the chutney to simmer for 45 minutes, or until it has thickened enough to stick to your spoon.

Decant the chutney into sterilised Kilner jars, seal while it's still hot to form a vacuum, and store. It will keep in the fridge for up to a month.

cook's tip... This chutney would pair beautifully with a good cheddar or Manchego cheese.

That Secret Shortbread

This is your go-to recipe for elevating your graze boards. Shortbreads are simple but enhance your creations because of their adaptability in taste, shape and texture. You'll be using this recipe over and over again, just like me - I couldn't keep this one a secret!

Preparation time: 30 minutes, plus 1 hour chilling | Makes 20 biscuits

ingredients

250g butter

125g caster sugar

375g plain flour

Optional Flavourings

1 lemon or orange, zested

50g chocolate chips

3 tbsp finely chopped fresh lavender

Optional Toppings

200g dark chocolate, melted

50g pistachios, crushed

method

In a medium-size bowl, cream the butter and caster sugar together until light and fluffy. Stir in the flour just until the mixture forms a dough. If you are using any of the optional flavourings to make lemon, orange, chocolate chip or lavender shortbreads, add them now.

Wrap the shortbread dough in cling film and gently press to flatten - this will make it easier to roll out when chilled. Leave the dough in the fridge for 30 minutes.

Roll out the chilled dough on a lightly floured surface until you have a sheet about 3mm thick. Take a cutter of any shape or size that you like. I have used a 6cm star cutter here. Cut out your shapes from the dough and carefully transfer the biscuits to a lined baking tray.

Now chill the biscuits in the fridge for another 30 minutes. This stops the shortbread from spreading in the oven, so your shapes won't turn out puffy. Meanwhile, preheat the oven to 160°c fan.

Place the chilled tray of biscuits into the preheated oven and bake for 8 to 10 minutes, or until the edges of the shortbread start to turn golden brown. Remove from the oven and cool on a wire rack.

If you are using the optional toppings, dip the cooled biscuits in the melted chocolate or drizzle over the top, then sprinkle with crushed pistachios if you like.

Cheese Straws

These cheesy pastry bites are so much tastier than shop-bought ones, and are so simple and fun to make. Add your favourite cheeses and seasonings for an individual flavour that you love.

Preparation time: 30-40 minutes | Makes 8-12

ingredients

375g ready-rolled puff pastry

2 tsp a little of everything seasoning (see recipe on page 158)

125g cheese, grated (such as cheddar, Lancashire or parmesan)

method

Line a baking tray that is approximately 30cm in diameter. Unroll the pastry and divide the sheet into two equal sections.

Sprinkle most of your cheese and the seasoning over one section of your puff pastry. Place the remaining section of puff pastry on top.

Lightly press the sheets together with a rolling pin until they stick, then scatter the remaining cheese on top of the pastry.

Cut the sandwiched pastry sheets into strips about 3cm wide. Twist the ends of each strip twice to create the 'twirl' on your cheese straws and then place them in the fridge for 15 minutes. Meanwhile, preheat the oven to 200°c.

Remove the chilled cheese straws from the fridge and place them on the lined baking tray. Bake for 20 to 25 minutes, or until golden and firm to the touch. Remove from the oven and place on a wire rack to cool.

These cheese straws can be stored in an airtight container for up to 2 days, but are at their best within 2 hours of being baked.

cook's tip... All hard cheeses work well with this recipe, so try using your own favourite for a more individual take on these cheese straws.

Morgan's Scones with Jam Butters

My good friend Morgan makes the most delicious bakes, and his scone recipe is the best I have ever tasted. For me, scones and jam are the quintessential British summertime grazing treat. Pair these little beauties with any of the recipes in this book, or serve on their own for a mid-afternoon treat.

Preparation time: 35-40 minutes | Makes about 20 mini scones

ingredients

500g plain flour

28g baking powder

90g caster sugar

125g butter

2 eggs, plus 1 yolk

135ml whole milk, plus an extra splash

50g sultanas (optional)

method

Preheat your oven to 190°c fan. Sift the flour, baking powder and sugar into a medium-size mixing bowl. Cut the butter into approximately 2cm cubes and add to the mixture.

Coat all the butter with the dry mixture and use a butter knife to continue chopping the butter into smaller pieces and coating them with the flour. Once you have very small cubes of butter, use your fingers to gently rub them into the dry ingredients until the mixture is a breadcrumb-like consistency.

In a separate bowl or jug, whisk the whole eggs and 135ml of milk together, then pour them into the dry mixture. Using your hands, bring the mixture together until the dough is fairly soft but not wet. It should not be firm in texture, as the moisture is what makes the scones fluffy once baked. Add the sultanas at this point if desired.

On a lightly floured surface, roll out the dough to a thickness of 2cm, being careful not to use too much flour as this will make the scones heavier. Dip a 4cm round cutter into some flour and cut as many scones as possible out of the dough. Transfer them carefully to a lined baking tray.

Whisk the egg yolk with the extra splash of milk, then brush this mixture over the tops of the scones with a pastry brush. Be careful to prevent any egg wash dripping down the sides of the scones, as this could stop them rising evenly. Bake the scones in the preheated oven for 12 to 15 minutes.

Serve the scones warm with fresh Cheshire clotted cream and jam, or jam butters (see below).

Jam Butters

Simply combine 100g of softened butter with 4 tablespoons or more of your favourite jam. I have used strawberry, raspberry and blackberry before which all work well. Place in a ramekin and store in the fridge to spread on your scones, toast or sandwiches.

Pumpkin Spiced Almonds

These sweet, crunchy nuts add a taste of autumn to your boards. Make double the amount, add them to a pretty jar, tie on a ribbon and it's the perfect homemade gift.

Preparation time: 20 minutes | Makes 300g

ingredients

6 tbsp maple syrup

60ml water

250g brown sugar

300g almonds

For the pumpkin spice mix

¾ tbsp ground cinnamon

¼ tbsp allspice

¼ tbsp each of ground nutmeg, cloves and ginger

For the cinnamon sugar mix

200g granulated sugar

2 tbsp ground cinnamon

method

Combine the ingredients for the pumpkin spice and cinnamon sugar mixtures in separate small bowls. Put the maple syrup, water and brown sugar into a large saucepan and stir gently.

Place the pan over a medium heat and continue to stir gently until all the sugar has completely dissolved. Add the pumpkin spice mix and stir until that has dissolved too.

Add the almonds to the pan and coat them with the mixture until all the nuts are completely covered. Continue to stir them until the remaining syrup has been absorbed, taking care not to burn the sugar on the bottom of the pan.

Remove the pan from the heat and tip the nuts onto a baking tray lined with baking parchment. Separate the almonds with forks while they are still warm, otherwise they will all stick together in a large clump.

Sprinkle the pumpkin spiced nuts with the cinnamon sugar while they cool, tossing them carefully to coat each one without sticking them together.

These will stay fresh for approximately 1 week in a Mason jar.

cook's tip... These are great for adding to a trail mix as well as snacking on with boards.

Cinnamon Candied Pecans

These nuts add another level of flavour to your boards. Pop them in a pretty jar, tie on a ribbon and you also have the perfect homemade gift.

Preparation time: 15 minutes | Makes 300g

ingredients

100g brown sugar

235g granulated sugar

2¾ tbsp cinnamon

60ml water

300g pecans

method

Combine the brown sugar with 35g of the granulated sugar, three quarters of a tablespoon of cinnamon and the water in a large saucepan. Stir gently and place on a medium heat until all the sugar has dissolved completely

Add the pecans to the pan and stir again to coat them with the mixture until all the nuts are completely covered.

Continue to stir the mixture over the heat until all the sugar and water has been absorbed by the nuts, taking care not to burn the sugar on the bottom, then remove the pan from the heat.

Place the nuts onto a baking tray lined with baking parchment. Separate the candied pecans using forks while they are still warm, otherwise they will stick together in a large clump.

Combine the remaining 200g of granulated sugar and 2 tablespoons of cinnamon, then sprinkle the pecans with the cinnamon sugar while the nuts are cooling. Toss or shake them to coat evenly.

cook's tip... These candied pecans will stay fresh for approximately 1 week in a Mason jar.

Tatton Trail Mix

I love to walk around my local area in Cheshire, and Tatton Park is a family favourite. This easy trail mix is made with all your favourite ingredients to elevate your graze boards further and give you the perfect outdoor snack.

Preparation time: 5 minutes

ingredients

Mini marshmallows

Chocolate chips

Pumpkin seeds

Dried cranberries

Pistachios

Hazelnuts

Almonds

Pretzels

Mini chocolate peanut butter cups

Cinnamon candied pecans (see recipe on page 176)

method

Take a muffin tray and fill each hole with the ingredients of your choice. You can use different colours of marshmallows and white, milk or dark chocolate chips if you like: whether there are three ingredients or twelve is entirely up to you.

Simply scoop your chosen and measured ingredients into a bowl and mix with a spoon. You can add ramekins of your trail mix to graze boards, or enjoy it as a great snack on the go.

The beauty and simplicity of this is that you can put in whatever you enjoy, and even add seasonal treats to your trail mix depending on the time of year. Play with colours, flavours and themes but most importantly, have fun!

cook's tip... Try making a seasonal trail mix by adding chocolate Santas for Christmas, mini eggs at Easter or any other seasonal sweet treats.

Frosty Cranberries

I love the combination of tart and sweet in these cranberries. They don't last very long in our house! I buy the cranberries in bulk over winter and freeze them to enjoy all year around in cocktails or accompaniments for my boards. You can also try this recipe with blueberries.

Preparation time: 24 hours | Makes about 350g

ingredients

350g fresh or frozen cranberries

1 litre water

200g granulated sugar

method

Wash the cranberries thoroughly. Heat the water in a large saucepan, then add 100g of the sugar to the pan and let the sugar dissolve.

Gently stir the cranberries into the syrup, then simmer for about 5 minutes. Remove from the heat before they split and leave the cranberries in the pan of syrup for a few hours.

Remove the cranberries with a slotted spoon and place on a wire rack to dry. I usually leave them overnight because they are really sticky at this point. Dry until they are tacky to the touch.

Test one of the syrupy cranberries by rolling it in the remaining 100g of granulated sugar. The sugar should stick to the cranberry effortlessly, but if it clumps, then they are too wet and need a little longer to dry. Take your time and roll the cranberries in the sugar in batches of two or three.

To serve, place the frosted cranberries in a glass bowl and add a sprig of rosemary for a festive feel.

cook's tip... Decant the syrup into a Kilner bottle and save for a festive cocktail.

Dried Orange Slices

These orange slices add a hint of festivity to your boards and are also useful for presents, adding to cocktails or for decorations. You could also try this with other citrus fruits such as lemons or limes.

Preparation time: 5 hours | Makes about 20

ingredients

5 large oranges

method

Preheat the oven to 120-140°c. Meanwhile, wash and dry the oranges thoroughly.

Using a mandoline, slice the oranges so they are less than half a centimetre thick.

Place the orange slices on a wire rack with a lined baking tray underneath to collect the juice. Cook in the preheated oven for around 5 hours, or until dry and crispy to the touch. Turn the slices occasionally while cooking, and keep checking to make sure they don't turn brown.

Remove the dried orange slices from the oven and leave them to cool completely. Store in an airtight container at room temperature for up to 1 month.

For an extra treat, dip the dried orange slices in melted dark chocolate and sprinkle on some crushed pistachios. Leave to set before serving.

cook's tip... These orange slices make lovely decorations for your seasonal garlands.

Chocolate Hazelnut Dip

This sweet chocolate hazelnut dip is a great alternative to melted chocolate or shop-bought jars of chocolate spread. It's so easy to make and doesn't last very long in our house! Perfect for your graze boards, but also for spreading on toast, adding to sandwiches or dipping fresh fruit in.

Preparation time: 15-30 minutes | Makes 125g

ingredients

250g hazelnuts

100g good quality dark chocolate (the higher the % of cocoa solids, the better)

2 tbsp maple syrup

1 tbsp vanilla essence

Pinch of salt

method

If you're using hazelnuts with skins, start by toasting them in the oven for 15 minutes on a medium heat. Tip the hot hazelnuts into a tea towel and rub to remove the skins. Alternatively, use blanched hazelnuts which have had their skins already removed.

Blend the skinned hazelnuts in a food processor for a good 10 minutes, until the oil is released from the nuts. Meanwhile, break up the chocolate into a heatproof bowl and melt in the microwave for about 1 minute in short bursts, checking frequently to make sure it doesn't burn or seize. When the chocolate is almost melted, remove from the microwave and stir until smooth.

Pour the melted chocolate over the blended hazelnuts and stir to combine, then add the maple syrup, vanilla and a pinch of salt to taste. Mix thoroughly until well combined. If the consistency is too thick, add a little hot water to make the dip smoother. Store in the fridge for up to 2 weeks, if it lasts that long!

cook's tip... This recipe makes a healthier alternative to shop-bought chocolate spreads.

Chocolate Bark

The secret here is to use the best quality chocolate you can find. Have fun making your own bark which will elevate your boards and add seasonal hints to your creations.

Preparation time: 20 minutes

ingredients

Good quality chocolate of your choice

Embellishments of your choice, such as:

Rose petals

Pistachios or hazelnuts

Dried cranberries

Sugar strands

Freeze-dried raspberries or strawberries

Edible glitter

Sweets

Popcorn

method

Line a baking tray with parchment or baking paper. Break the chocolate into a microwaveable bowl and heat in short bursts, checking and stirring it every 30 to 60 seconds until melted.

Pour the melted chocolate onto the lined baking tray to create a slab of your preferred thickness. Scatter over the embellishments to add flavour or seasonal fun and play around with colours and textures to make your own beautiful designs. You could also melt two different chocolates, such as white and milk, then swirl them together for more interest.

Allow the decorated slab to cool at room temperature, then use a sharp knife to cut the chocolate bark into shards.

This easy and fun recipe can be used to make lovely homemade gifts in clear bags or jars, as well as beautiful additions to your boards.

cook's tip... Have fun experimenting with different nuts, dried fruit and food colouring to make your perfect bark.

Chocolate Salami

This indulgent sweet treat is perfect around Christmas time and will keep for a couple of weeks in your fridge. You can add all your favourite nuts and biscuits to make it more personalised.

Preparation time: 30 minutes, plus setting overnight | Makes about 20 slices

ingredients

225g dark or milk chocolate

100g digestive biscuits

80g amaretti biscuits

90g butter

150g caster sugar

2 tbsp cocoa powder

80g nuts of your choice (hazelnuts, pistachios or almonds work well)

Icing sugar, to decorate

method

Start by breaking up the chocolate into a heatproof bowl and microwaving for about 2 minutes, checking frequently to make sure it doesn't burn or seize, until melted. Stir well until smooth.

Put all the biscuits in a sealable bag, lay on a flat surface, cover with a tea towel and bash with a rolling pin until you have a rubble of evenly-sized pieces.

In a separate bowl, cream the butter and sugar together. Whisk the cocoa powder into the melted chocolate, then gradually add the butter and sugar mixture to the melted chocolate.

Stir in the crushed biscuits and nuts, make sure everything is thoroughly combined, then allow the mixture to firm up before handling which should take around 20 minutes.

Lay out a large sheet of cling film or tin foil on a clean surface. I find tin foil easier to handle personally. Tip the chocolate mixture into the centre of the sheet and roll into a log by pushing in one direction and using the tin foil or cling film to wrap the mixture, until you have a cylinder about 25cm long. When the log is shaped and covered, twist the ends of the foil or film to keep all the contents tightly in place. Leave the chocolate log in the fridge overnight to set.

Remove the set chocolate log from the fridge, unwrap the foil or film, place on a serving plate and dust with icing sugar so that the chocolate log looks like salami.

You can leave it like this, or tie string around the chocolate log so that it looks even more like salami. To do this, measure out a piece of string that is 6 times the length of the log. Make a loop with the string and feed the log through the loop, then form another loop around the salami, feeding the other end of the string through. Do this every few centimetres until you reach the end and then tie the string around the end of the chocolate log.

Slice the chocolate salami on a chopping board when ready to serve.

INSPIRED GRAZING

©2021 Laura Billington & Meze Publishing Limited

First edition printed in 2021 in the UK

Printed and bound in the UK by Bell & Bain Ltd, Glasgow

ISBN: 978-1-910863-78-7

Written by: Laura Billington & Katie Fisher

Edited by: Phil Turner

Designed by: Paul Cocker

Photography by: Danny & Jenny Shortall,
Shortall Shots Photography, www.shortallshots.com

Illustrations by: Nicole Billington, Instagram @nicoleune

Baked recipes by: Morgan Mole, That Secret Ingredient,
www.thatsecretingredient.co.uk

PR: Emma Toogood, Ben Travis

Contributors: Natalie Billington, Suki Broad, Michael Johnson

Published by Meze Publishing Limited

Unit 1b, 2 Kelham Square

Kelham Riverside

Sheffield S3 8SD

Web: www.mezepublishing.co.uk

Telephone: 0114 275 7709

Email: info@mezepublishing.co.uk

No part of this book shall be reproduced or transmitted in any form or by any means, electronic or mechanical, including photocopying, recording, or by any information retrieval system without written permission of the publisher.

Although every precaution has been taken in the preparation of this work, the publisher and author assume no responsibility for errors or omissions. Neither is any liability assumed for damages resulting from the use of this information contained herein.

SO WHETHER YOU EAT OR DRINK OR WHATEVER YOU DO,
DO IT ALL FOR THE GLORY OF GOD.

1 CORINTHIANS 10:31